Coaching Basketball's Multiple 2-1-2 Full-Court Zone Press

John Kimble

ISBN: 978-1-60679-175-2
Library of Congress Control Number: 2011927531
Cover design: Studio J Art & Design
Book layout: Studio J Art & Design
Front cover photo: ©James DeCamp/Southcreek Global/ZUMApress.com

Coaches Choice
P.O. Box 1828
Monterey, CA 93942
www.coacheschoice.com

Dedication

There is an old saying: "Basketball has been very, very good to me." This saying fits very well for me in that I have had the privilege of meeting and getting to know some great people through the game of basketball. I have met many outstanding people through all of the players, the managers, the trainers, the statisticians, the film-takers, the parents, boosters, other support people, basketball officials (yes, even the officials), opposing coaches, and particularly coaches on my own staffs. Many different characteristics and traits have been exhibited through these various coaches I have had the pleasure of meeting. I have come to know many coaches who are dedicated to the game of basketball and to their players. I have had the pleasure of getting to know many coaches who are hardworking and very good technicians in teaching the fundamentals of the game. I have had the opportunity of meeting coaches who are tremendous teachers of the nuances of the game. I have come to know many coaches who are outstanding motivators of their players and other coaches. I have gotten to meet coaches who are loyal and faithful to their players, their coaching staff, and their school. I have been fortunate to meet coaches who are generous and share their time, their skills, and their experiences with other coaches. I have been able to meet coaches who are family men and have their priorities in order. Some of these coaches have great senses of humor and have such unassuming attitudes that shows the class and poise that they possess. I have enjoyed the privilege of meeting coaches who are honest, personable, and show class and humility in both victory and defeat. I have had the privilege of knowing some coaches who have demonstrated great amounts of courage and dignity in the middle of great distress and upheaval. These coaches have preached and believed in many of the outstanding characteristics that all of us should possess. Some coaches whom I have been able to meet can also be living examples to their players and to anyone who is fortunate to observe in them the qualities that they believe in.

But the one coach I can think of who not only possesses all of these traits and characteristics just mentioned (as well as others), but who is a shining example of these qualities, is Coach Don Meyer.

I have had the privilege of meeting Coach Meyer years ago through one of his former college players, who had nothing but the highest degree of respect of Coach Meyer as a coach, a teacher of life, and as a person. In one short, two-day period of being introduced and visiting with him, Coach Meyer became a strong influence in helping me start writing coaching books and eventually making some coaching DVDs. A couple of months later, I experienced one of the most outstanding performances by a coach I have ever observed in one of Coach Meyer's one-man coaching clinics. After just those two meetings with Coach Meyer, he then helped provide me with the information and knowledge on how to start the entire procedure in having a coaching book published. This advice is from a highly successful college basketball coach helping a high school coach who was basically a stranger. How many coaches, how many people would do that while living in today's world?

After I wrote my first two books (*The Basketball Coaches' Complete Guide to Zone Offenses* and *The Basketball Coaches' Complete Guide to the Multiple Match-Up Zone Defense*), I then received more support from Coach Meyer by his writing of very positive testimonials of these two books. This led to the writing of other books and even more increasing support by Coach Meyer writing the foreword of a third book. Throughout the entire process of my writing five books and the production of several DVDs, Coach Meyer has remained a constant source of encouragement and support to me. His encouragement to me came while still being a highly successful coach in a very successful college basketball program. His encouragement came while producing his own highly popular and valuable coaching DVDs. His encouragement to me came despite his own personal car accident and subsequent severe medical problems as well as he then continued recovering from injuries and countless surgeries to still coach basketball in a winning way.

Coach Meyer's professional career is one to behold being the all-time leader in coaching wins in NCAA men's basketball history with over 900 victories in the unbelievable 38-year tenure. But his professional coaching record of wins and losses almost tarnishes the immeasurable success he has accomplished in setting an example and being a leader of young men over the years in coaching. The basketball coaching world will not be what it is when Coach Meyer retires. Fortunately, the human race will still benefit with his countless contributions.

Coach Meyer is the ultimate teacher not only in basketball, but in life. He is the only basketball coach of the hundreds of coaches I have heard throughout the years who has spoken on how a coach can and should improve his personal life mentally, physically, and morally. I have witnessed from Coach Meyer some of the most unique ways and methods of motivating and teaching his players (and anyone who has the opportunity to be around him and to learn from him) to not only be better basketball players, but to be better people.

Therefore, I am honored to dedicate this book to Coach Meyer. I am glad that I have had the opportunity to meet Coach Meyer; he is one of the most remarkable men I have ever met and one of the best basketball coaches of all time. I am proud to call Coach Meyer a friend—a true friend.

Acknowledgments

This book is dedicated to all of those who have influenced my basketball coaching life and to all the committed basketball coaches who have spent countless hours at coaching clinics, reading books, and "X-ing and O-ing" it with their colleagues. I have been a player, a fan, a teacher of the game, a student of the game, a coach, and a lover of the game. As a student and a coach of the game, several influences have impacted my coaching beliefs. These influences range from summer basketball camps, coaching clinics, coaching textbooks and written publications, videotapes, observing other coaches' practices, and the countless informal coaching clinics with many other coaches trying to learn just one more drill, defense, or play.

Personal influences in my coaching life have come from many of the most top-notch coaches of the game: The Iowa Basketball Camp (Lute Olson and Scott Thompson), The Doug Collins Basketball Camp (Doug Collins and Bob Sullivan), The University of Illinois Basketball Camp (Dick Nagy and Lou Henson), The Indiana Basketball Camp (Bob Knight), The Dick Baumgartner Shooting Camp (Dick Baumgartner), The Washington State University Cougar Cage Camp (George Raveling, Tom Pugliese, Mark Edwards, and Jim Livengood), The Snow Valley Basketball School (Herb Livesey), The Notre Dame University Basketball Camp (Digger Phelps and Danny Nee), The Illinois State University Basketball Camp (Tom Richardson), The Millikin University Basketball Camp (Joe Ramsey), Eastern Illinois University (Don Eddy), The Purdue University Basketball Camp (Lee Rose), The Oregon State University Basketball Camp (Ralph Miller and Lanny Van Eman), The Troy State University Basketball Camp (Don Maestri), The Maryville (TN) College Basketball Camp (Randy Lambert), and The Kansas State University Basketball Camp (Jim Wooldridge, Mike Miller, Jimmy Elgas, Charles Baker, and Chad Altadonna). Just a few of the most memorable and outstanding speakers I have heard at some of the many coaching clinics I have attended have included: Coach Lute Olson, Coach Doug Collins, Coach Hubie Brown, Coach Bob Knight, Coach Dick Nagy, Coach Don Meyers, and Coach Rick Majerus.

The most outstanding authors of coaching books have included Coach Del Harris, Coach Dean Smith, Coach Bob Knight, and Coach Fran Webster. Coach Lute Olson, Coach Hubie Brown. Coach Don Meyer and Jerry Krause, Coach Del Harris, and Coach Dick Baumgartner have been authors of some of the most outstanding videotapes I have observed and learned a great deal. Coaching colleagues with whom I have worked include Doug Collins, Brian James, Gerry Thornton, Benny Gabbard, Steve Gould, Bob Sullivan, Norm Frazier, Tom Wierzba, Steve Laur, Ron Roher, Will Rey, Mike Davis, Dennis

Kagel, Don Eiker, Bob Trimble, Dave Toler, and Ed Butkovich. I was fortunate to always be involved with tremendous coaching staffs with outstanding coaches, who were even more outstanding as people and friends to me than as coaches. These good friends were outstanding people such as Benny Gabbard, Mitch Buckelew, Scott Huerkamp, Phil Barbara, Chris Martello, Don Tanney, Les Wilson, Al Cornish, Ron Lowery, John Lenz, Doug Zehr, and Ken Maye. To all of these people, I say, "Thank you for your loyalty, commitment, hard work, and effort!"

I would like to say thanks to the many players I have coached, to the extraordinary non-player students who were big parts of the basketball programs—the managers, the student statisticians, the film-takers, the student athletic trainers, and student helpers. I hope that I conveyed to each and every one of them the fact that they were important parts of the program and that they all deserved credit for the successes of their basketball programs that they were a part of.

I want to also say thank you to the adults whom I have met and become friends with in the different communities where I have coached. These are people who participated in the development and the successes of the basketball programs where I coached. These people were contributors, supporters of the program, faithful fans, and loyal friends. Some were parents of players, while some were parents of students, and some were just fans of the game. These people include Bob and Ro Flannagan, Ed and Roseanne Moore, Ron and Mary Roher, Dick and Sharon Payne, Don and Bev Hiter, Dave Gregory, Norm Frazier, John and Pam Russell, Ken and Judy Sunderland, Fred Prager, Mark Henry, Carlan and Dee Dee Martin, George Stakely, Charles Owens, Dutch VanBuskirk, Kelly Stanford, Junior Robertson, Bobby Johnson, June Carter, Greg Cadenhead, and so many other good people.

This book is also dedicated to those who have influenced my personal life. I was raised by inspirational parents who always taught me to go the extra step, to never be satisfied until the job was done right. I hope I have succeeded in accomplishing that goal with the writing of this book. My wife, Pat, was my biggest source of encouragement to write this book. She was my constant positive reinforcement and support. My daughter Emily and son Adam also were sources of personal encouragement, who helped me continue this endeavor. My two brothers, Joe and Jim, also offered support as I slowly progressed through the ordeal of organizing and writing. Also my parents, who were always positive role models and constant sources of encouragement and support. Gerry Thornton, longtime friend and fellow student of the game, has affected my coaching career probably more than any other person; while Benny Gabbard was the one person who got me started in my junior college coaching career and showed great faith and confidence in me in my first years of coaching junior college basketball. Coach Gabbard was the one coach who influenced me to adopt the "speed game" style of play while coaching together at the junior college level. Coach Don Meyer, who has been a helpful, encouraging and supportive friend as well as a tremendous example in being a great coach as well as a person. Jerry Krause (friend, coach at Gonzaga University, author, and an invaluable source of information) also was of great help and encouragement, as was Kevin Newell (former senior editor of *Scholastic Coach and Athletic Director*), supporter and friend, Murray Pool (former high school coach and current publisher of *Basketball Sense*, friend, and source of information), and Mike Podoll (editor of *Winning Hoops* basketball magazine).

Foreword

It has been my pleasure to have known Coach John Kimble for the past 30 years. I have enjoyed watching him progress from an enthusiastic young coach to a wizened veteran coach. He has always been a student of the game, and he has demonstrated a knack for creative and effective approaches to playing the game.

His latest book, *Coaching Basketball's Multiple 2-1-2 Full-Court Zone Press*, is a great example of this. His attention to detail and the strategic placement of the players makes it simple to grasp the defensive concepts of the press. What I found to be unique in his approach to playing a pressing defense is that he incorporates innovative and creative concepts that make it hard for an offense to prepare for the press. The offensive team must confront many different looks and principles. He covers many different scenarios that can occur during the game and how they can be countered by a team's defensive alignment and each individual defender's responsibility. In addition, he provides some provocative and insightful teaching points to help the players read the offense and determine what the other team is trying to do against the press.

This book is based upon many years of coaching experiences, observations, and tinkering to provide the best overall approach to playing an effective press defense. I highly recommend it to a coach looking for something that gives his team a competitive edge in a game where every decision a player faces can make the difference between winning and losing.

Mark Edwards
Head Men's Basketball Coach
Washington University in St. Louis

Contents

Introduction

A successful defensive system should have several similar traits that a successful offensive system possesses. Being fundamentally sound is the first trait for both systems. Another trait is that both systems will only be as strong as their weakest links. Both systems should be aggressive, but always under control. Both systems should put players in positions where they will succeed. Both systems should align personnel where they can maximize and highlight their individual skills and talents.

Even though the defensive side of the ball is diametrically opposite of the offensive side of the ball, a good coaching staff must counter the traditional attitude that the offensive team's players are the actors and the defensive team's players are the reactors. A good defensive team attacks and forces the offensive team to react and try to counter the initial assault. This approach is a drastic change in attitude but one that is paramount in building a strong defensive mind-set and overall aggressive system. If a defensive-minded coaching staff can teach, coach, and sell the theory that the defense acts and the offense reacts, his defensive team has passed the first hurdle.

Another trait that a good defensive team can take from an offensive system is that a defensive team can also be multiple in its attacks on the opposition and therefore be even more unpredictable. This makes that defensive team more difficult to prepare for and therefore more difficult to play against.

The perception to many coaches that a team that plays multiple defenses is subject to mental errors and confusion because of its alleged complexity is as inaccurate as the notion that an offensive team cannot execute the same basic entry/play out of different offensive sets. The idea that an offensive team can execute basically the same quick-hitter play out of different sets is much more common than the same idea that a defensive team can defensively run a quick-hitter (what, defensively, is called a "stunt") out of different (defensive) alignments. If a team can do this on offense, why can it not do the same on defense?

Many offensive systems use multiple offensive quick-hitter plays, highlighting individual offensive player's talents and skills. Why can't a defensive system be built in the same manner?

Many offensive plays are also designed to attack perceived weaknesses of the individual opponent by forcing defenders out of positions in which they are comfortable, forcing defenders to do things they are not accustomed (or possibly coached) to doing. Why can't a defensive system be created to attack the opposition's offense in the same manner?

Countless offensive systems exist where the offensive play does not produce points but will easily flow into a continuity offense to keep the attack going on the opposition. Why can't a defensive system be able to attack in the same manner?

This book outlines a defensive system that can accomplish all of these characteristics of many offensive systems.

Momentum is a big part of athletics, because of the positive mind-set that can exist for the team that achieves the momentum. A question can be asked: "Which comes first—success or momentum?" It is believed because the game is "so mental," once just a small amount of success takes place, momentum and self-confidence can then be created. That momentum and self-confidence can then carry over to lead that team to even more success, which can then lead to even more momentum and so on. Just a little success can be the seed that plants the momentum that then can grow into more success.

An individual player or a team can have some success because of self-confidence, and that little success can create more confidence, which leads to more success, and the momentum builds and builds to more and more success. An offensive team can "get hot" and seemingly make every shot it takes. Why can't a defensive team acquire the same type of momentum? That defensive type of momentum is called a "defensive spurt."

Defensive spurts are the occasions when a defensive team, particularly a pressure-type defensive team, has a series of defensive possessions where the defensive team rattles the offensive team and creates a flurry of turnovers. The defensive spurt does not have to last but a couple of possessions. I stress to my pressing teams that one opponent turnover is usually followed by another, but there can definitely be more than one defensive spurt in a game.

The entire game can be broken into 10 or 11 three-minute "mini-games." If a defensive pressing team can "win" just one or two of these mini-games via defensive spurts, and then just break even in the remaining mini-games, the game will be won by the pressing defensive team. If a defensive team can create a couple of defensive spurts in each game that produces even the slightest point scoring advantage and then play the rest of the game at close to a break-even score, that team most likely will win the ballgame.

The more often a team applies pressure defense, the better chance a team has in creating defensive spurts. A team can afford to apply defensive pressure more often in a game if that team very rarely or never gives up easy scores after the pressure defense fails. So, a primary objective of any full-court pressure defense is to never give up easy scores to the opposition. If the opposition earns the score, so be it, but the opponent's press offense must be forced to make good plays if and when they score—never on the defense's mistakes.

A defensive team that is efficient and productive in its press defensive package also possesses a mental edge that other teams will not have. Regardless of how poorly the offensive team is shooting and in its overall performance, regardless of how far behind that team may get, the team that has developed a successful full-court press system will always possess the quiet inner confidence of "No matter what, we still have a chance to win." Often, that positive attitude mind-set of the pressing team can also weigh heavily on the opposition's offensive team.

If a team is losing late in a game and time becomes a factor, that team will most likely be forced to apply full-court pressure to try to erase the deficit. If that team has not used the full-court press beforehand, the players on that team will instinctively know that the coaching staff does not have much confidence in the full-court pressing game. If that coaching staff had confidence in that phase of their game, they would have used it earlier and more often, rather than in just a last-ditch effort to salvage a game. If the press has not been used beforehand, the players also will not have confidence or will not possess the experience and practice of utilizing the press. The deficit that forced the press to be used will very well likely remain and possibly will even grow.

Full-court zone press defenses must be a necessary ingredient to basketball teams, and while they don't necessarily have to be used all of the time, every team should have at least one zone press that can be periodically used throughout the course of a game.

Every basketball team has its own unique set of strengths and weaknesses. A good coaching staff must find those overall strengths and weaknesses. The weaknesses must be strengthened and minimized while the strengths must be improved as well as utilized. Some form of pressure defense must be adapted to fit the style, the needs, and the strengths of a basketball team while blending in with the coaching staff's philosophy on how the game should be played.

A full-court press defense does not have to force the opposition's offense into a turnover that then results in an immediate score for the defense every time. That is an obvious goal, but an impossible task. A full-court press defensive system can produce many subtle by-products:

- Press defenses or any defense at any level (be it full court, 3/4 court, half court, or sagging half court) should be considered and thought of as a unique but still a valuable form of offense.

- Defense is a constant where offensive shooting can be fickle. Great offensive shooting isn't always there night after night. Your defense should never have an off night.

- Opponents' fatigue, both mental and physical, is caused by a defensive pressing team wearing the opposition down. That fatigue can affect the opposition's own defense as well as its offensive performance over the course of a full game.

- Full-court pressing can most definitely speed an opponent's offense into an up-tempo game that they are unaccustomed to and therefore might be more uncomfortable with, resulting in turnovers and poor offensive (as well as poor defensive) play.

- Particular defensive stunts from specific full-court presses might actually be used to slow down an opponent who wants a faster-paced game. Some stunts allow the defense to control the tempo better as well as keep the opposition's offense under more control. Therefore, press defenses can help control the tempo of a game, be it to speed up or slow down an opponent. A defensive team that can dictate tempo has a huge advantage in determining the outcome of a game.

- Pressing defenses that create turnovers obviously limit the opposition's offense to a fewer number of shots, which greatly lowers the chance of the opposition from scoring as many points. The actual turnover also provides the defensive team with not only more shot opportunities but better shot opportunities. Shots resulting from opponent's turnovers likely will result in a larger number as well as higher percentage shots closer to the basket than your best and most precisely designed half-court offenses. These shot opportunities most likely will be closer range shots with those shots being less contested. Even if the shot is missed, the likelihood of your team getting more offensive rebounds also increases because of the possible number advantage as well as the organizational advantage. Your team's increased chances of offensive rebounds means greater chances for scoring (even if the original shot is missed after creating the turnover).

- Pressing defenses causes opposing coaches and team to spend valuable (limited) practice time in preparing to face the different press alignments/sets as well as the various (quick-hitting) pressing stunts your team can execute. This preparation time then cannot be utilized on other phases of the game, thereby minimizing the opposition's overall preparation and, ultimately, its success.

- Pressing defenses can accentuate and highlight individual defender's specific skills and talents to maximize your players' skills.

- Conversely, pressing defenses can probe, discover, and attack an opponent's offensive team weaknesses as well as individual offensive opponent's specific individual weaknesses. Once discovered, these team and individual weaknesses can be exploited and capitalized upon.

- Win as many "mini-games" as possible, and break even in the others. Let your press defenses help contribute.

This book is designed to help coaches find the full-court press defense(s) that can fit their team's needs. I hope that every coach can successfully make this book a valuable instrument in developing or reshaping their team's overall defensive package and schemes.

About the Companion DVD

This book includes a supplemental DVD that reinforces the concepts and techniques discussed in the book. As the book is broken down into chapters covering various topics, the DVD tries to fit those topics into actual on-court demonstrations of working with and teaching/coaching players.

Subsequent to the filming of the DVD, a few modifications were made to this zone press defensive system, and the book has been updated accordingly. Following are a summary of the changes:

- The original 2-1-2 zone press (called the 3 press in the DVD) has been renamed 2 press.
- The original 3 press face referred to in the DVD has been renamed the 3 press.
- The original 2-2-1 zone press (called the 2 press in the DVD) has been eliminated from this defensive package. If a coach still wants to implement the 2-2-1 press, it should be called the 4 press.

The only difference between the three or four zone presses discussed in the book and DVD should be to move only one defender. That defender should be called the Monster, and should be positioned as follows:

- In the 1-2-1-1 press (called the 1 press), the Monster is located defending the opposition's inbound passer.
- In the 2-1-2 press (now called the 2 press), the same Monster would be the defender in the exact middle of the four other defenders.
- In the (newly called) 3 press, the same Monster would stay in the middle of the press, with the other four defenders remaining in the same locations with the same responsibilities and the same required techniques.
- If the 2-2-1 press (now called the 4 press) is determined by the coaching staff to be included in the overall defensive package, the same Monster would be the lone defender in the third line of defenders initially defending the basket.

To enhance the book's material, the DVD can be viewed as a whole entity or in individual parts after each individual chapter of the book has been read. The actual practice and teaching of the concepts on the practice floor in the DVD should also provide a more comprehensive explanation of the history and how the press was actually developed. Every aggressive defensive team should possess this information.

1

History of the Development of the 2 Press

Early in my coaching career, I became an advocate of full-court zone presses for many reasons. I saw the need for a team to adapt an aggressive and pressure type of full-court defense that should not only be used late in a basketball game when the team is down by several points, but also to control tempo of the game, and to instill an aggressive mind-set both defensively as well as offensively.

I wanted teams to have that aggressive and hustling mind-set. I wanted our teams to instill fear, doubt, and confusion in every team we played. I also took parts of my football coaching philosophy and experiences to help develop my basketball coaching philosophy. I learned that a defense did not have to be a passive and reactionary entity. I tried to develop basketball teams to have an aggressive and attacking attitude with their defenses.

Full-court pressure used from the beginning and used sporadically throughout the game until our opponent's offense scored easy baskets from our press defenses was proactive, not reactive. Then, we would either make adjustments or simply call off the press for a while before then putting the press back on. It still amazes me how an opposing basketball offense can solve a full-court press defense for a while, and then later in the same game when the press is reapplied, the same offense will collapse under the same press defense(s).

The football coach in me persuaded the basketball coach in me that full-court (as well as half-court) basketball defenses could initiate attacks on the opposition's basketball offenses just like a football defense could have defensive stunts that could confuse a football offense with different aggressive types of action that were disguised. Some of the defensive action would stifle the run, while other action could rush the quarterback and discourage the pass. Football taught me that certain football defenses and action could aggressively take away an opposing football team's strength, whether it was the run or the pass, and make that team attempt to utilize the weaker part of their offensive attack. The defense could then capitalize on the weakness of that offensive team once it was discovered and avoid the strengths of that team once they also were realized. Football helped me develop the attitude that the defense does not have to sit, wait, read, and react to the opposition's offense. With defensive overplays, aggressive schemes, and several stunts that were disguised, that football defense could become the aggressor and make the football offense the team to be passive, cautious, and reactionary.

An aggressive and defensive-minded basketball coaching philosophy was born and has continued to be modified and hopefully improved upon ever since. Along with that mind-set came the attitude and philosophy that basketball defenses (as well as offenses) could become multiple to make that team unpredictable, difficult to scout and therefore difficult to play against.

The idea of breaking down certain aspects of the overall defense (and the opposition's offense) into more simplified breakdown drills that could enhance every player's understanding as well as hone all of the necessary skills needed for overall success was borrowed from the football coaching mentality.

The 1-2-1-1 full-court zone press (shortened to be called the "1 press") became the first and the primary press our defensive teams used. As a multiple defensive coach, the natural progression then led to our teams also developing the 2-2-1 full-court zone press (called the "2 press") as the secondary zone press used in our early defensive pressing scheme. We would use the 1 press quite often to see the ways our opponents would attempt to attack the zone press.

In addition to our use of defensive full-court zone pressure, our teams also faced opponents that used one or both of these popular and frequently used presses themselves. As a result, our coaching staffs studied not only the ways that opponents executed both of these defenses but also the press offenses that opponents used to try to attack our full-court pressure.

Not only did we use the 1 press more frequently than the 2 press, we faced the 1 press more often than the 2 press. We acquired more of an idea and working knowledge of the 1 press. One of the biggest beliefs we acquired in our experiences with full-court zone presses is the majority of offenses against the 1 press would position their offensive players in a 2-1-2 offensive set. The idea was then created to use the 1 press with a hard and aggressive trap on the ball while taking away both advancing passes down the ballside sideline and in the middle of the zone press, while being very conscious and looking for the long, diagonal skip pass. This approach gives the opposition's offense only the reversal pass as the most likely to be completed successfully. We noticed most press offenses ended up in a 2-1-2 offensive alignment after the ball was reversed. These particular offensive spot-up positions were not chosen by the opposition by accident. These positions are the natural gaps against the 1-2-1-1 zone press.

Another philosophy developed over the years is that we would like to implement some ideas that are possibly somewhat unique and a little different so that opposing teams would have to prepare exclusively for us. By having to put a special attack against our press, the opposition would naturally not be as well-prepared, which would help make our team's performance more productive and efficient.

This idea consists of using a somewhat different type of a zone press defense against an opponent's press offense. This technique not only can be confusing to the opposition, but the fact that a portion of the 10 seconds the opposition's offense must use to realign itself can also be a significant factor in the defense's performance.

We became a fan of the 2-2-1 full-court zone press for many reasons. One primary reason was because it was a great complement to the 1-2-1-1 full-court zone press as well as giving the defense an opportunity to be more multiple and less predictable. Another reason was that it attacked offenses in a completely different manner. Instead of aggressively and immediately trapping the initial pass (like the 1 press does), the 2-2-1 full-court press can allow the initial inbounds pass and then wait to attack the offense by fanning the dribbler down the sideline and rotating a backline defender up with the ball defender to double-team trap the dribbler along the sideline. This additional press then provided the defense another way of being the actor and forcing the opposition's offense to being the reactor.

As valuable as the 2-2-1 full-court zone press could be to the overall defensive package that a defensive-minded coach could integrate, the 2-2-1 full-court zone press had some weaknesses that concerned us. One of the biggest weaknesses we felt in the 2-2-1 full-court zone press was that the middle of this press defense was somewhat vulnerable and could be attacked. By attacking the middle of the press, the offense could possibly gain a numerical advantage in attacking their offensive basket.

The second weakness was the concept that made one of our backline players rotate up toward the basketball and actually away from the basket he was to defend. We wanted our press to attack the offense but we did not want to give up easy and quick baskets. Rotating the original safety—our first basket protector—away from that area he was to defend concerned us a great deal.

A third weakness was that the original safety of the 2-2-1 zone press could easily be seen in this rotation toward the ball by the opposition's ball handler as he dribbled down the sideline toward his basket (and to potential pass receivers). We did not like the idea that a dribbler could see his potential trapper running at him and also see the potential interceptor (to his sideline pass) rotating up and out toward the pass receiver. The 2-2-1 zone press had to have a defender rotate back to protect the middle somewhat and also have a second defender rotate back to protect the basket now left unprotected.

But after studying the 2-1-2 full-court zone press, we believed its weaknesses paled versus the weaknesses of the 2-2-1 zone press. While the 2-1-2 full-court zone press not only had the same strengths and benefits of the 2-2-1 press, it actually had many more strengths and had eliminated the three major weaknesses we felt the 2-2-1 full-court zone press possessed. This reasoning compelled us to remove the 2-2-1 press from our defensive package and to implement the 2-1-2 full-court zone press as our new (and improved) 2 press as the complement to the 1-2-1-1 full-court zone press. (From there, the idea of the 3 press, which will be discussed in subsequent chapters, came into play as still another way for our defense to confuse and attack the opposition's offense.) A key strength of the 2 press package is that this defense has the possibility and potential of adding defensive stunts to its overall defensive scheme. Stunts can give any full-court zone press different plans and ways of attacking the opposition's offense, which makes the 2 press even more aggressive, more unpredictable, and more confusing for the opposition's offense to be able to figure out and counter. The 2 press package could also contain as many as four different stunts, depending on the physical and mental capabilities of each year's squad.

The 2 press defensive stunts also have some of the same defensive concepts that the full-court run-and-jump press defense possesses. The in stunt and the out stunt both have distinct characteristics that are fundamentally sound defensive techniques for either of the two press defenses. When used in the context of the 2 press, these defensive fundamentals and techniques can possibly have even more success than when used in the run-and-jump defense.

Therefore, the 2-1-2 press evolved from our analysis of the 1-2-1-1 press and the 2-2-1 press. It developed from our interpretation of both their strengths and weaknesses as defensive coaches as well as how we viewed the presses when we faced them against our defensive opponents.

We believed that the common impression of most coaches is that the 1 press is much more aggressive, particularly by trapping the first inbounded pass, while our new 2 press is a passive and more cautious press that confuses and attacks sideline dribblers. We also believed that the 2 press could be utilized by using the 1 press to set up opposing zone press offenses as well as using the 2 press alone (along with its various stunts.)

Defensively, we wanted to take the best of both worlds to create an aggressive press that protected the middle while still having the opportunity to sometimes trap the first pass as well as to have the capability to surprise-trap the dribbler when *and* where we wanted to trap him. All of these defensive goals and objectives can be accomplished with the 2 press. We incorporated the 2 press with our overall offensive and defensive philosophies of building a multiple defensive system that was simple for our players to learn, understand, and execute, as well as easy for us to communicate with the players about the adjustments, but still appearing to be a complex and complicated attacking defensive system that our opponents had questions in preparing for and more difficulty in trying to solve and defeat.

In summary, we decided to use the 2 press and its stunts as our primary full-court zone defense for the following reasons:

- It uses a multiple defense philosophy.
- It embraces an "actors, not reactors" philosophy that is very aggressive in nature.
- The opponents' offensive spot-ups are actually filled by the rotating defenders.
- The opposition is facing a type of zone press that is possibly somewhat different than what they are accustomed to facing.
- This somewhat new and different zone press manipulates offensive opponents into positions that would be the most unproductive locations they could possibly be, as well as into offensive counteractions that should be unsuccessful in their attack.
- It offers the option of adding different stunts (different methods of attacking the opposition's offense) that can highlight defenders' skills and talents as well as attack opponent's individual offensive weaknesses.
- It also allows the defense to take advantage of the opponent's overall team weaknesses in their attempt to react and counter the defensive attack.

2

Terminology, Points of Emphasis, and Teaching Phrases

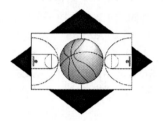

Following are some of the defensive terms, definitions, theories, and concepts that an aggressive and successful defense must have in order to be the defensive power it can become:

- T-I-P-S (Techniques-Intensity-Position-Stance)
- The defense can be the actors, and not the reactors
- Tightside of the court
- Wideside of the court
- Ball stance
- Push-push
- Fanning the dribbler
- Use the sideline and the timeline as extra defenders
- Dribble alley of the offense
- Bluff and retreat
- The L-trap with the feet
- No lines/no splits
- Cross-face, and trace the ball
- Chest bump
- An out-of-control dribbler
- Sprint and wolf the dribbler

- Passing line
- Helpside
- Ball-you-man-in-your-area flat triangle
- See the ball and the man (in your zone area)
- The farther you are from the ball, the farther you are from your man (in your zone press area)
- Pistols stance, head on a swivel (to see the ball and the man in your area)
- Jump toward the ball
- Don't wait, but anticipate and sprint to where the ball is going to land
- Physically, you are here; but mentally, you are there
- Long arm (of a defender)
- Shoot the gap

The acronym "T-I-P-S" is used as a teaching tool for the defense:
- T: (Proper) *Techniques* by each defender
- I: (High levels of) *Intensity* of each defender
- P: (Proper) *Position*/location for each defender
- S: (Correct defensive) *Stance* by each defender

If individual defenders can execute the proper *Techniques*, maintain a high level of *Intensity*, and always have the correct *Positioning* and location regardless of where the ball is and where they are on the court, and always have the right defensive *Stance*, then those defenders will be successful. If individual defenders are successful in solving their own individual defensive puzzles, the team also will solve its puzzle (Figure 2-1). Therefore, the defensive team's overall performance will be a much greater success.

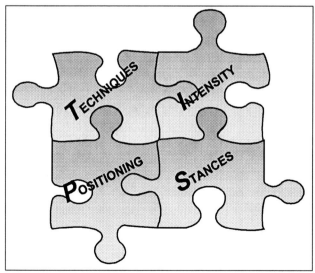

Figure 2-1

The defense can be the actors and not the reactors. This theory is the overall defensive philosophy that could (and should) be used for whatever type of defense is used, regardless of whether it is full court, 3/4 court, or half court. No rule in basketball states that the offense has to have the advantage of being in control and that the defense must wait, read, and then decide on how to react to the movement of the opposition's offense. Instead, you want your defenders to be the aggressors. You want your defense to force the action—to be the actors, to dictate so the opposition's offense must adjust to your initiatives and force them (and not your defense) to become the reactors. This philosophy actually can simplify matters for the defense; it can give the defense more initiative, more aggressiveness, more confidence, and ultimately, more success.

The tightside of the court is defined as the side of the full court that the offensive Trigger (the man taking the ball out-of-bounds to initiate the opposition's press offense) takes the ball out-of-bounds. If the 1 press is utilized, the Monster (M3) first pressures their Trigger before then rotating to trap the first receiver with his tight wing teammate. This trap cannot be done successfully unless the ball is passed to the tightside because the Monster (M3) would have too far of a defensive run from pressuring their Trigger to properly trapping a ball handler on the far side of the court (with the wide wing). This philosophy of initially trapping the inbounds pass from the tightside only coincides with the defensive (as well as the offensive) philosophy that players are expected to play hard and to play smart. Good coaches should only place players in situations where those players have opportunities to succeed. The majority of offensive players, and thus the majority of offenses, are right-handed. Therefore, most defenses have their tightside on their left side of the defense (Diagram 2-1).

The defense's wideside is the side of the court opposite of the tightside. Therefore, if you are executing the 1 press, you only have the Monster (M3) trap with the wing on the defense's tightside of the court and not the wideside. This gives the Monster only reasonable expectations he can execute. You should always have high expectations of your defenders, but do not have unreasonable expectations. Having the Monster (M3) pressure the ball out-of-bounds to help discourage a quick long throw and then expecting that same defender to go to the wideside of the court (which is the farthest distance from him) and successfully trap the ball with the wide wing (WW1) is an unreasonable attitude and a defensive maneuver that will not be successful.

For this reason, both sides of the court must be defined. Then, a clearly defined assignment for the Monster on the initial inbounded pass must be a reasonable one. That is the reason why the wide wing plays the receiver in his area differently than the tight wing plays the receiver on his side of the floor. If the ball is actually inbounded to the wideside, teach the player to treat it as if the ball started on the tightside and was then reversed to the wideside. Those techniques will be discussed later in the book.

The 2 press and the 3 press also have a tightside and a wideside, but where the initial inbounded pass is made is not as significant as it is when the 1 press is used.

Diagram 2-2 shows the tightside and the wideside of the press. WW1 and R4 line up on the wideside, while TW2 and B5 operate from the tightside, and M3 controls the middle.

The *ball stance* for the zone press is the stance that defenders on the basketball always use to influence and pressure the basketball. It is an overplay that almost always fans the basketball toward the outside. In the full-court setting, the location of the ball itself immediately takes away one of the offensive player's triple threats: shooting. Pressuring the basketball with the proper techniques can help take away the offensive player's second threat: passing. By taking away an offensive opponent's shooting and passing, the offensive opponent is left with just one of his three basic threats: dribbling.

Overplaying the dribbler in a specific manner can allow the defense to discourage the pass while also dictating where the dribbler can actually go with his dribble. That direction of the dribble is now predictable and easier to defend as well as actually being where the overall defensive plan wants the ball to go. As previously discussed, fanning the ball can provide the defensive team with an extra defender: the sideline. This overplay on the ball can also force the dribbler to locations advantageous to the defense, while detrimental to the offense.

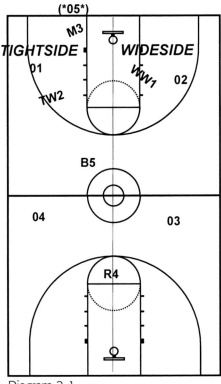

Diagram 2-1

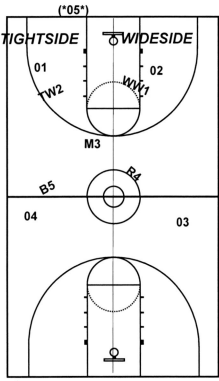

Diagram 2-2

The *push-push* defensive technique is only for the ball defenders who are controlling and dictating where the dribbler is going to go. This technique utilizes the defender using the lead foot to step in the direction that the defender wants to go. This slide movement is powered by the trail leg and foot by that player actually pushing hard in the direction he wants the dribbler to go. This is where the "T" is utilized in the defensive T-I-P-S.

Fanning the dribbler is a term used by all ball defenders of any of the press defenses. It is simply an overplay used by the ball defender (TW2) to not just persuade but to aggressively force the dribbler to the outside down the sideline. This play can allow the defensive team to also use the sideline (as well as the 10-second timeline) as extra defenders, giving the defense a hypothetical seven defensive players to five offensive players numerical advantage. This action can provide the defensive pressing team with the means of being able to be more aggressive and more successful. Diagram 2-3 shows the 2 press with the in stunt being executed. The in stunt will be covered in Chapter 5.

Use the sideline and the timeline as extra defenders. This technique and coaching point of emphasis benefits the ball defenders who fan the opposition's ball handler to the outside down the sideline. The sideline and sometimes the 10-second timeline can help limit and decrease the area that the opposition's offensive players can utilize. This concept or theory can greatly benefit the defensive team without actually using an additional defender on the ball. If the original ball defender can fan or influence the dribbler to the sideline, that sideline can serve as an extra defender before M3 then jump-traps the dribbler after TW2 has forced the dribbler to change directions. Diagram 2-3 illustrates the in stunt on the tightside of the court.

The *dribble alley* is the imaginary dribbling space between the actual dribbler, the defender, and the sideline. The closer both the dribbler and defender get to the 10-second timeline, the narrower the dribble alley should be. As will be shown later, this approach makes for a higher success rate of the second line defender of the 2 press out and the 3 press out stunt rotating up to trap with the original ball defender. If the 3 press in stunt is being executed, the original ball defender (either TW2 or WW1) is the defender who has to narrow the dribble alley so that he is the defender that must actually get ahead of the dribbler to eventually force the dribbler back toward the middle, where the Monster (M3) applies the jump trap (Diagram 2-3).

The *bluff and retreat* terminology should be used by the ballside defenders on both the front and second line of either the 2 press or the 3 press. This technique is only performed by the second line defender on the ballside and is used to exemplify the all-important defensive concept "defenders can be the actors" while forcing the offensive dribbler to become the reactor. The second line defender on the ballside (either B5 on the defense's left side or R4 on the defense's right side) bluffs up the sideline toward the ball handler as if he is running up to jump-trap the ball with the original ball defender before then retreating from the confused dribbler.

This feigning of the sideline trap could lead to the defense *not* actually trapping with these two defenders, or it could possibly lead to a different type of sideline trap. Another possibility is that the bluff and retreat action could also lead to the backline defender actually bluffing and then retreating before the Monster (M3) jump-traps during the execution of the 2 press in or the 3 press in stunt. This bluff and retreat can also help the ball defender bring the dribbler under control. Diagram 2-4 illustrates B5 bluffing (up) and then retreating (back) before finally rotating up and trapping with TW2 just on the backcourt side of the timeline. Note that the trap could be set on the frontcourt side of the time line, dependent upon the coaching staff's preference.

The *L-trap with the feet* teaching/coaching phrase is a major focal point that must be constantly stressed to all players by all defensive coaches. This phrase will constantly remind both trappers that the positioning of both of their feet is a very important technique. The inside foot of both defenders should be placed together at a 90-degree angle to help discourage and ultimately prevent splits of the trap via an offensive dribble and/or an escape pass.

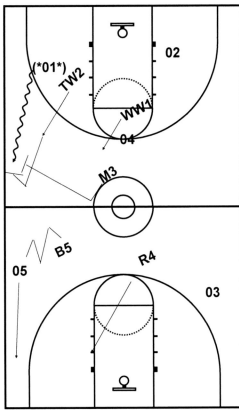

Diagram 2-3

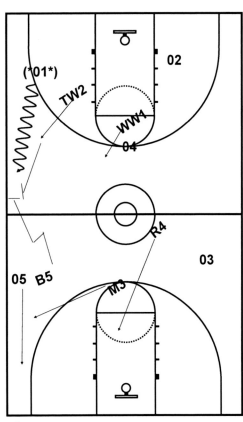

Diagram 2-4

Integrated closely with the L-trap with the feet coaching point of emphasis is the phrase, *no lines/no splits.* Both trappers must always adhere to this teaching phrase. If the ball handler defeats the press by either splitting the trap via dribble or escapes the trap with some type of a pass, the offense has just defeated not one, but two defenders. That means that two defenders are now behind the level of the ball. These two defenders must get back to the new ball level. Diagram 2-4 illustrates the trap set by both TW2 and B5 with both defenders having the inside foot interlocking so that no dribbler could split that trap.

The phrase *cross-face and trace the ball* is another essential phrase that describes the defensive technique that all ball defenders, particularly double-teamed trappers, should utilize. Utilizing these techniques properly will compel defenders to apply maximum pressure on the ball and not reach in, thereby having minimum chances of fouling (and therefore letting the ball handler off the hook).

Another defensive technique that allows defenders to pressure the basketball with minimal chances of cheap reaching in fouls is called the *chest bump.* This coaching point is simple to teach. It reminds all defenders on the ball to not reach in on the ball, but to still apply maximum pressure by bumping the offensive player with the chest. This type of physical contact often is not considered and called a foul by the officials. In Diagram 2-4, both TW2 and B5 are to use the correct trapping techniques with their feet, their arms and hands and also their chests.

An *out-of-control dribbler* is defined as an offensive opponent with the basketball who has increased his dribble speed to defeat the ball defender. An out-of-control dribbler can work to the defensive team's advantage if this type of dribbler has been channeled into a particular dribble alley near the sideline so that the designated off-the-ball defender can rotate up to trap the dribbler. The bluff and retreat technique can be used by a second line defender to help confuse the dribbler as to if and when the trap is coming and therefore help cause a turnover.

With the press defense using the 10-second timeline, the zone press can have two different looks in any of the three various zone press defenses, with both looks having two different sets of advantages and disadvantages. Defensive coaches must weigh the advantages and disadvantages to determine if they want to dictate one side or the other to trap, or if they simply want to allow the defensive team to randomly trap on either side of the court.

All three of these choices all have strong merits and possible negative results. If the ball is stopped (or trapped) on the backcourt side of the timeline, the two major factors for the defense are the following: the offense has only 10 seconds to advance the ball across the timeline (and that time period could very well be about to expire), and the defense would still have the entire court to defend since the ball has not crossed the time line.

If the dribble is killed on the frontcourt side of the timeline, no 10-second time limit would be running, but a new five-second closely guarded time limit would begin. Much more importantly, the amount of the court that the defense must try to cover is cut in half, making it easier to look and guard potential pass receivers and allowing all off-the-ball defenders to step up closer toward the passing lines of each potential pass receiver.

Sprint and wolf the dribbler is a defensive term for all defenders who were passed up by the advancement of the ball. This advancement could occur by the dribbler or from the dribbler's pass. Those defenders (TW2 and M3) should immediately sprint and attempt to get to the new ball level. As they are hustling back, these defenders should sprint after the ball handler and look to back tip the ball as he comes up from behind the ball handler. This technique can be a very effective way to force turnovers. Even if the wolf back tip is not successful, the defenders who were sprinting during the chasing of the ball are more inclined to get back to the new ball level.

The first defender who then faces the escaped dribbler should stalk the dribbler to slow him down and contain the ball. He should approach him cautiously so as not to force him to veer off to either side and ultimately dribble past him. He is to contain the dribbler and give each wolf defender a chance to wolf and get to the new ball level. Diagram 2-5 displays O2 splitting the trap set by TW2 and M3 with a dribble. These two defenders must then race along beside the dribbler, trying to tip the ball from behind (wolfing). WW1, B5, R4 drop back to stalk and contain the dribbler and also protect the basket to discourage O2 to continue with his dribble.

The *passing line* is the imaginary line between the basketball in O1's hands and the offensive counterpart that each defender is responsible for. For example, the imaginary line between O1 with the ball and O2 is one of the passing lines described. Also shown are those same types of passing lines from O1 to O3 and from O1 to O5. This line forms the longest side of the (imaginary) triangle in the teaching concept of good positioning for all off-the-ball defenders (Diagram 2-6).

Helpside is the half-court man-to-man term used for all off-the-ball defenders that are located on the offense's weakside of the court away from the basketball. It is termed "helpside" instead of "weakside" to remind defenders not guarding the basketball that they can position themselves toward the basketball to provide "help" for the ball defenders and thus bring more defensive pressure on the opposition's ball handlers. The helpside line can be described as the (imaginary) vertical center line that runs the length of the full court.

The *ball-you-man flat triangle* is primarily a half-court, man-to-man defensive concept. It serves as a teaching point of emphasis for coaches to show the proper positioning of all off-the-ball defenders regarding their man and the basketball. With

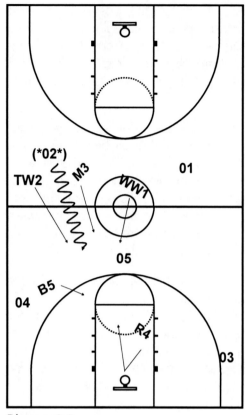

Diagram 2-5

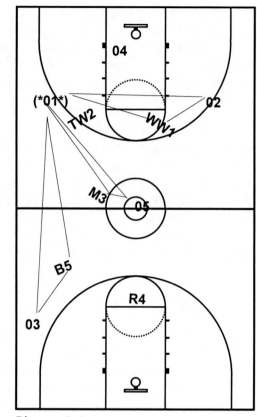

Diagram 2-6

five offensive players and only one basketball, a defender is guarding an opponent who does not have the ball 80 percent of the time. Therefore, off-the-ball defense is of vital importance. These defenders must guard their own man yet provide support defense to the lone ball-defending teammate. Theoretically, this technique allows the actual ball defender to be able to pressure the basketball more since he knows he has a support defense behind him if he gets beaten on dribble drives and penetration.

Since this discussion concerns zone press defenses, this man-to-man defensive term has been modified to be *ball-you-man-in-your-area flat triangle*. This simply means that each zone press defender who is not pressuring the basketball does not have one specific opponent as his sole responsibility but any offensive player who is in his actual zone area.

Each off-the-ball defender is to create an imaginary triangle between the actual ball (*ball*), themselves (*you*), and that offensive player in their zone area (*man in your area*) while utilizing the passing line as one of the three sides of his own specific triangle. The flatter the triangle, the closer to the actual passing line that defender is. Zone press defenders should be about two full steps off of the passing line in forming their particular flat triangle (Diagram 2-6).

The point that is literally between the actual position of the opponent with the basketball and the opponent that does not have the ball is the location of that defender. That third point of the (imaginary) triangle is the actual defender, and that location is determined by two factors. One factor is how far off of the passing line does the coaching staff want the defender to be? That question is somewhat answered by the fact that each off-the-ball defender has to be able to have peripheral vision to be able to always *see the ball and the man (in your zone area.)* A particular defender might have to step farther away from the passing line simply to improve his peripheral vision and be able to see both that man in his (zone) area as well as the ball.

The *farther you are from the ball, the farther you can be from your man (in your zone area)* concept is also a derivative from the half-court man defensive concept "the farther you are from the ball, the farther you are from your man." This invaluable concept and technique insures that an off-the-ball defender is sagging off of his man enough to accomplish two defensive objectives. The first purpose is to be a major support force that will always be able to provide defensive help to the ball defender when he applies ball pressure and is sometimes beaten on dribble penetration and drives. The second purpose is to allow that support defender to be far enough from his man so that he will have time to react to whatever his opponent does. Having enough reaction time makes the off-the-ball defense much stronger in countering and neutralizing any offensive action the off-the-ball offensive player executes. Again, the man-to-man concept is modified slightly so that it can easily adapt to the zone press defensive scheme. Note that the triangle between the ball and B5 is a longer triangle, and that B5 is further from O3 because he is farther from the ball compared to the triangle of M3 (Diagram 2-6).

These modified defensive concepts are tailored to fit the zone press defensive package and fall under the realm of the P in the defensive acronym T-I-P-S while other defensive concepts and points of emphasis fall under the S, for stance. These important concepts will now be discussed.

Now that positioning and locations of zone press defenders has been explained, a defensive concept for all off-the-ball defenders is the type of stance that these players can use to make the defense more successful. Even though this phrase was made primarily for man-to-man defenders, *pistols stance/head on a swivel* is a phrase that can be used as a great teaching point to successfully teach and train defenders using the zone press. Either four (if only one ball defender) or three (if the ball is being double-team trapped) defensive players are off the ball and defending men in their respective zone areas. If this type of stance is good enough for man-to-man defenses, it is good enough for zone press defenses. These defenders should already understand and be applying the positioning/location concepts and techniques that have just been discussed. This particular teaching point helps teach and train off-the-ball defenders in regard to their actual stances. Each defender should be set up in a *ball-you-man-in-your-area flat triangle* approximately two full steps off of the passing line as their positioning point of reference. All defenders not on or trapping the ball should have a defensive stance that has both hands clenched in somewhat of a fist with the index finger of each hand extended as if each hand were a pistol. Then, one pistol should be pointing toward the ball and the other pistol toward the man in their zone area. This technique causes each defender to concentrate and be aware of that offensive opponent as well as having constant vision of the basketball. Another man-to-man defensive phrase that should appropriately be applied to zone press defenses is *see the ball and see the man (in your zone area.)*

Jump toward the ball is a common man-to-man defense coaching point that can and should be utilized for all zone press defenders. Any time a zone press defender is originally on the basketball (either as a solo defender or as part of a double-teaming trapper) and the basketball has escaped out of the defensive pressure, every off-the-ball defender should then instantly jump toward the new location of the ball to help create his own new and up-to-date (imaginary) ball-you-man-in-your-area flat triangle. These new triangles are a must for continued defensive success for any type of defense (man, zone, or zone press) at any point on the court (half- or full-court level.)

Don't wait, but anticipate and sprint to where the ball is going to land is a defensive phrase that should be used by coaching staffs to emphasize that all trappers (regardless of what zone press is being utilized) should not watch the escape pass and wait to where the ball is going to land, before rushing toward the ball. Instead, defensive players should predict where the pass is to land and then hustle to that anticipated location before or as the ball actually arrives.

Still another defensive phrase that is used to emphasize to defenders how anticipation and thinking can be such a major contributor to the individual defender's quickness and speed is: *physically, you are here, but mentally, you are there.* The quicker and the better the anticipation a defender possesses, the more efficient and successful the overall defensive pressure is, making each defender less of a reactor when the ball actually is advanced in one form or another. A team that utilizes defensive overplays, defensive stunts, and multiple defenses is a team that can apply the concept of the defensive team being more of the actor and not the reactor. This anticipation coaching phrase is still another way of making the defensive team quicker and more aggressive.

The *belly-to-belly and long arm (of a defender)* is a defensive term for all off-the-ball defenders that somewhat joins the defensive term with the pistols stance term, except this defensive technique should be used more by defenders who are guarding an offensive player who is only one pass away from the basketball. This technique allows that particular defender to be more aggressive in denying the pass to that specific offensive pass receiver, without committing as many defensive fouls. The belly-to-belly part of this phrase means that when the defender gets very close to the offensive receiver, he should turn into the receiver with his body facing the receiver. This technique will allow the defender to become a parenthesis and avoid some of the contact with the receiver, while still seeing the offensive player. The "long arm" part of the phrase simply means that the long arm is the arm of a defender that is closest to the actual passer. Using the long arm technique helps the defender maintain that belly-to-belly stance with the offensive receiver and helps form the parenthesis in the defender's denial stance. Diagram 2-7 illustrates the approximate body positioning of the five defenders. Just imagine the long bar in the middle as the defender's back, and the direction of the opening of the symbols as the direction the defender is taking.

Shoot the gap is a term for any off-the-ball defenders who are rushing for a potential intercepted pass. M3 and TW2 are rotating in anticipation of intercepting a pass. One defender (M3) has anticipated the upcoming trap by WW1 and R4 on the opposition's ball handler (02) and also where the ball handler will pass the ball (supposedly to an open offensive opponent (03)). TW2 is the defender who is rotating back to protect the middle area after M3 has rotated down the sideline. R4 has rotated up to trap the ball with WW1 on the execution of the out stunt (Diagram 2-8).

For the defender to be more successful in intercepting this type of pass, defenders must use the appropriate T-I-P-S. The understanding and use of the techniques of T-I-P-S will result in more interceptions and more overall defensive success.

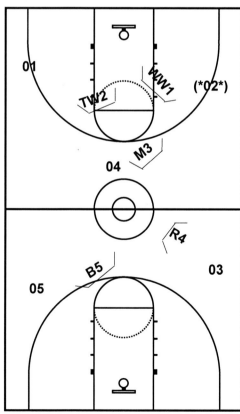

Diagram 2-7

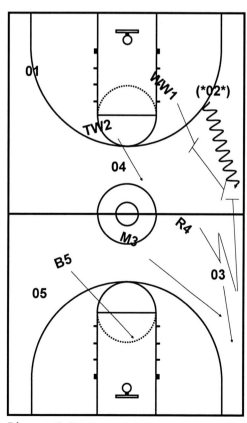

Diagram 2-8

3

Placement of Personnel for the Zone Presses

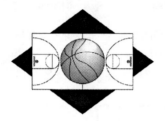

In general, when executing the 1 press place the small forward (03) as the Monster (M3) on the opposition's Trigger, who is attempting to inbound the basketball. Assume that the point guard (01) is the best ball defender you have, with the shooting guard (02) being your second-best ball defender. In the 1 press, encourage the ball to be inbounded on the tightside of the court—the side of the court where the opponent's Trigger inbounds the ball.

After the inbounds pass is made on the tightside and the ball is quickly trapped, you want to be able to have the 1 press take away all passes that advance the ball down the court. This will most likely be at the expense of having to give up the reverse pass to the middle lane area or to the wideside of the press, but at least behind the original ball level. You want to have the opportunity to trap the initial inbounded pass and take away any advancement of the ball via dribble or pass and give up only a pass that is reversed to the opposite side of the court that is actually further from the opponent's offensive basket than the original location of the inbounded pass. Be willing to concede that pass, and expect that the pass will be successfully made. Therefore, position the defenders accordingly, knowing that the most likely second pass is on ball reversal.

Since most teams are right-handed, you want your second-best ball defender to defend the most logical player (01) to receive that inbounded first pass. That defender is called the tight wing (TW2).

The defensive wing opposite the tight wing is called the wide wing (WW1). Obviously, you want to place him on the side opposite of the opponent's Trigger. In this way, once the ball is trapped (by TW2 and M3) and more than likely the opposition escapes that first trap with a reversal pass (to the wideside); you then would have your best ball defender (01) on the ball.

Defensive coaches should place the slowest post player (05) as the backline defender on the tightside (the offense's right side) and call him the Bandit (B5). Align the quickest post player (04) on the backline on the "wideside." Call this defender the Robber (R4). Place the best ball defender (01) on the wideside because the ball will eventually be coming down that particular side of the court the majority of the time. You want to position the defenders in locations where they can be more valuable to the team (Diagram 3-1).

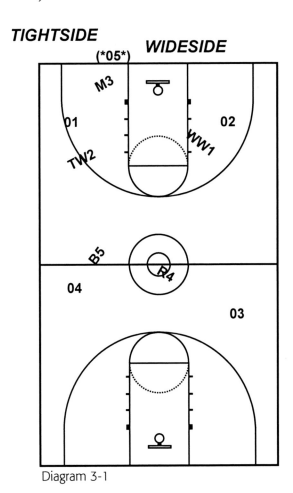

Diagram 3-1

If the decision is made to tandem up the backline players to truly set up in a 1-2-1-1 defensive press alignment, place the Bandit (B5) nearer the actual trap and near the opponent's backcourt edge of the center jump circle. Place the Robber (R4) further from the initial trap and near the top of the key of the opponent's basket (Diagram 3-2).

The proper placement of personnel demonstrates a philosophy of literally putting players (either offensively or defensively) into the locations where they have the best opportunities to succeed. It also fits the old saying: a defense is only as strong as its weakest link. All five defensive players are located where they can maximize their skills and talents, while they can also minimize their defensive weaknesses. These locations and assignments greatly enhance the chance of individual defensive success, and it gives the overall team defense a much better opportunity of defensive accomplishments.

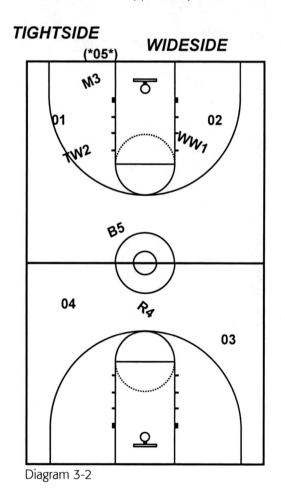

Diagram 3-2

The most unique item in the placement of defenders in this press system would be the fact that the quickest defenders of both the perimeter (X1) and post types of players (X4) basically start on the side of the court opposite of where the defense first encourages the opposition to inbound the basketball, particularly when executing the 1 press. If the 2 press or the 3 press is being employed, the defense may want to encourage the ball to initially go to the so-called quicker side of the court.

For defenders to be more versatile and therefore more valuable to their team, defensive players must learn the concepts as well as practice the specific defensive techniques of more than just one defensive position. Just like on the offensive side of the ball, because of injuries, foul trouble, or other reasons, defensive players could very well be forced to play other positions in the various defensive schemes.

So that a team is not forced to abandon the various presses because of a lack of defensive pressing depth, coaching staffs must analyze the entire squad for defensive replacements. To analyze the team properly, defensive coaches must find two or three players in each of the five defensive positions for each of the full-court zone press.

Another advantage of the full-court zone press defensive package is the countless similarities within all three zone presses. Many concepts, techniques, and needed skills are very similar in each of the three zone presses. If the presses are properly taught and practiced by incorporating various breakdown drills, all three presses are somewhat being practiced simultaneously. This approach makes the teaching (by the coaching staff), the learning (by the players), and the practicing of the presses much easier and more time efficient.

Although many similarities can be found in the three presses, a team does not have to utilize all three zone presses to be effective. A coaching staff must also analyze individual players' mental skills to be assured that a team can mentally handle the possibility of a multiple zone press defensive package. The coaching staff must also analyze and evaluate the individual defensive players' physical attributes to see if one or two or all three presses fit their physical capabilities. These two assessments of the defensive players are very important, and that decision must be made with great care.

Building the Foundations for the 1, 2, and 3 Presses

A full-court defensive pressing system requires a huge amount of effort from both players and coaches. The entire coaching staff must believe in the system and convincingly sell every advantage of the pressing system to each player. Therefore, every player and every person involved in the team must have confidence and faith in their full-court press system.

Even though the full-court press defense is on the other side of the ball from the offense, this defensive system should have concepts that are very similar to the offensive concepts. Regardless of whether a team utilizes the 1 press (a 1-2-1-1 zone press), the 2 press (a 2-1-2 zone press), the 3 press (a face-guarding 2-1-2 zone press), or a combination of more than one of these full-court zone presses, many concepts and philosophies should be a part of a coaching staff's overall defensive scheme. These concepts and beliefs should be integrated within their half-court defensive package as well.

Full-Court Press Defense Concepts and Philosophy

- The primary concept for both the offense and the defense should be simply to put players in positions and situations where they can maximize their success, and conversely, to attempt to put the opposition into situations and scenarios where they will have the least amount of success.

- Coaches should analyze individual skills and talents of each player and place the defensive personnel in the defensive positions where they will be most able to improve and to succeed. A coach should be demanding of his players, but should not place unrealistic expectations and assignments on players where they cannot succeed.

- Coaches should simplify and then be able to have players specialize in their skills, talents, and techniques. Coaching staffs should disguise parts of the presses (or of the offenses) so that the perception to his players is that it is simple and easy for them to comprehend. The cosmetic changes can disguise those similarities so that the opposition's perception of the defensive package is multiple, complex, difficult to scout, predict, and therefore difficult to prepare to play against. Coaches could apply cosmetic changes to disguise offensive similarities as well.

- Coaches and staffs should analyze everything in both their defensive and offensive systems to have an idea of the weaknesses and strengths of that phase of the game as well as how opposing coaches will attack them. Countermeasures must then be developed and taught to his players to always stay one step ahead of the opposition, which is where the different defensive stunts and alignments come into play.

- A team that incorporates a full-court pressing system can give that team a unique type of mind-set. Defenses do not have to be the reactors that wait and attempt to defend the opposition's offensive moves. Instead, the defense can become the actors. The defense aggressively initiates and forces the action, making the offensive opposition the reactors. The offense waits and attempts to read and counter the defensive team's attack on their offense.

- This mind-set can give a basketball team a huge amount of confidence, giving it even more of an aggressive nature for its defense as well as carryover value into its offensive part of the game.

- Teams that utilize a full-court zone press defensive system can wear down opponents both emotionally as well as physically. Being pressed by a defensive team that utilizes different looks and different forms of attacks (stunts) can easily take a toll on that offensive team. When there is a momentary breakdown, things can deteriorate quickly for that offensive team. Defensive players should believe in the fact that defensive spurts occur in every game. One turnover by the opposition can easily be followed by a second and a third, especially if the defensive pressing team amps up the defensive pressure (while staying under control.)

- The press defense package could very well sometimes become a team's most efficient offense as well as always being able to give the team a mental and emotional edge over each opponent. A team's offense may not just have it some night, but a press defense package that requires energy, attitude, and intensity should be a constant and be there every night.

- Having a full-court pressing system presents many different advantages to the defensive team both on the defensive side of the ball as well as the offensive part of the game. Countless times, a good team can manage to win a game when the offense doesn't carry its share of the load on a particular night. The star scorer has an off night, or the majority of the team has an off shooting night. The shooting stats can be fickle, but the defense (as long as it has its share of attacking weapons) should never have an off night in the effort department. The defensive effort and defensive weapons can help will a team to a victory when offense lets the team down.

- Coaches should use similar concepts and teaching phrases of one part of the defense that has already been learned and developed in other parts of the overall defensive scheme.

- The press defense package must be used at least sporadically throughout the entire game—not only to come from behind late in the game in a desperate last-ditch effort to win the game. If used only at the end of the game, players will see that the press is not a valued and trusted weapon in the staff's eyes. That lack of faith in the press system by the coaching staff will be transferred over to the defensive players and their defensive performance will suffer. A team that finds itself behind late in the game and has not utilized a full-court pressure defense until it has been forced to will sense that the coaching staff has not had confidence in the team's defensive press and is only utilizing it because the time and score has forced them to use it late in the game. The team that does not use the press system until they are forced to use the press has not committed to the system and therefore most likely will not have the success it desires.

- The use of a full-court pressing system that is multiple in its various alignments and stunts will present more opportunities to beat the opponent's press offense.

- By using a pressing system that flows easily and smoothly from its offense, the defense has more occasions to beat the opponent's transition from their half-court defense to their designated full-court press offense, which is an organizational advantage over their opponents. If a team's offense can produce points, why can't that team's full-court press system do the same, especially when that pressing team causes turnovers and has the opportunity to then attack the opposition when they will not have the capabilities of being able to recover and reorganize to be 100 percent effective. The press defenses that are selected should have the capabilities to not only create turnovers but to also produce immediate high-percentage shot opportunities or at least to smoothly flow into their secondary fast break offenses. This smooth flow maintains a constant attack on the opposition's offense as well as its defense.

- Use full-court press defenses that are fundamentally sound in concept, that fit a team's defensive personnel's talents and skill, and fit the coaching staff's offensive and defensive philosophies.

- The full-court press defenses that are chosen should also have the capabilities to add various types of defensive stunts that are beneficial to the overall defensive scheme.

- Coaches should utilize and integrate concepts, theories, ideas, philosophies, and teaching/coaching phrases that have been previously learned and executed not only in other facets of the overall defensive package, but possibly in some of the offensive concepts.

- Offensively, half-court sets are best used where a specific play is run. If the play does not score, it places offensive players into offensive spot-ups, so that the offense can continue to attack the opposition with an offensive continuity attack. This offensive philosophy can and should be applied to the defensive scheme as well. Defensively, the different defensive alignments are the defense's set. The defensive stunt is similar to the offensive play. If the offensive play (or the defensive stunt) does not produce the results, it places personnel into proper spot-ups to continue the offensive continuity (or the press defense). This approach keeps the team constantly attacking the opposition. In other words, the offensive and defensive similarities are as follows: the defensive alignment is similar to the offensive alignment/set, the defensive stunt's likeness is to the offensive play/entry, and the defensive continuation of the zone press is similar to an offensive team's half-court continuity offense.

- On offense, a coaching staff can utilize an offensive set and various plays to highlight his team's overall special talents or to attack his opponents' general defensive weaknesses. Why can't a defensive-minded coach do the same thing when building his defensive package? A coaching staff should use different press alignments/sets and stunts to capitalize on the overall defensive alignments' strengths and particular opponent's offensive weaknesses they have discovered.

- Likewise on offense, a coaching staff can utilize various offensive sets and plays to highlight special individual offensive talents of one or more of his players or to take advantage of discovered weaknesses of certain opposing defenders. Why shouldn't or couldn't the coaching staff implement various defensive alignments and stunts to capitalize on individual's defensive strengths or an opposing individual's offensive weaknesses?

- If an offensive team can execute various plays and offensive sets to become less scout-able to the opposition, why couldn't or shouldn't a defensive coach use different alignments and/or stunts to be more multiple and less predictable? Being multiple on defense can easily cause more confusion to the opposition and require them to use more time to be devoted in preparation of your team's pressing system (Figure 4-1).

- Different stunts can be run out of the various different press alignments. The different presses and the different stunts put more pressure on the opposition to

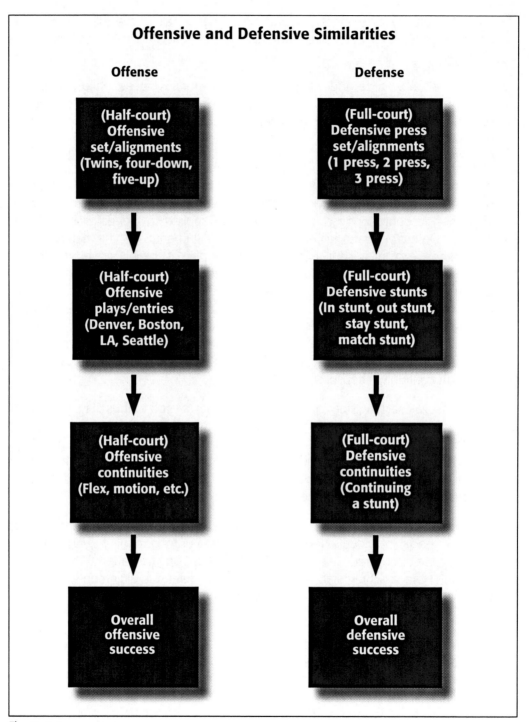

Figure 4-1

first survive the initial attack of the press, then the attack of the stunt, and then on into the particular half-court defense that your team employs should the opposition gets that far while still maintaining possession of the basketball. The opposition's offensive weaknesses can be exposed and taken advantage of, while the defensive strengths of the initial alignment or defensive personnel can be maximized.

The same stunts can be executed out of different press defenses. On offense, some offensive plays can be executed in the same manner out of various offensive sets, making the offense appear to be complex to the opposition, while actually keeping the package very simplified to its own players. Different defensive stunts can be run out of the same press alignment to serve as quick-hitting defensive attacks on the opposition's offense. These stunts again are designed to take advantage of the defense's strengths, to highlight individual defender's strengths, and to attack the weaknesses of the opponent's offensive press concepts (or opposing individual offensive player's weaknesses). The different defensive presses can be implemented to attack a particular press offensive concept or an individual offensive opponent. Opponents' offenses will first have to adjust to and survive the original full-court press, then the particular stunt (attack) employed, before then facing the half-court defense used.

- Teams that utilize all three zone presses are perceived as a complex defensive system. When drills are used for one particular press, the other presses are actually being worked on also. This approach gives the defensive team an advantage of being very time efficient in its preparation of its overall defensive package.

- Every full-court press offense exhibits some form of team weaknesses. A defensive-minded coach should study and analyze the particular styles of the press offenses that are being used against his team. A different press or a particular stunt may counter the offense's strengths and also capitalize on the offensive weaknesses. The various press offense's techniques that an opposing team uses need to be analyzed beforehand (via scouting previous games or tapes of games), including:
  ✓ Is there a designated Trigger of their press offense?
  ✓ Who is that designated Trigger?
  ✓ Does the opposition inbound the ball quickly?
  ✓ Do they look to quickly throw long?
  ✓ Do all offensive personnel align in the same general areas each and every time?
  ✓ Where do they place their two best ball handlers? Can those two offensive opponents handle the ball with both hands? If not, what is their weak hand?
  ✓ Do they start someone in the middle of the press defense?
  ✓ Does the opposition flash someone to the middle?
  ✓ Does the offensive opposition have an aggressive attitude and want to attack the defensive press or just survive the press?

✓ Do they have offensive finishers, if the press is defeated?

✓ Do they have any truly weak ball handlers, and where are they aligned?

✓ Can their post players handle the basketball? Can they pass well or dribble well, or are they a definite liability when in possession of the ball?

- Make sure all defensive players know their (defense to offensive transition) responsibilities and that those responsibilities and assignments can be carried out by each and every player.

- Coaches should sell to the defensive players that the presses will create turnovers and that the turnovers will in turn create shot opportunities for them (against an inferior defense that is disorganized and scrambling). But not all of your shots will be made, so excellent offensive rebound opportunities will still exist. Make sure that offensive rebounding responsibility rules are clearly defined. Make sure there always remains a defensive tailback, even after an offensive conversion from a steal off the press.

- If a coaching staff elects to be multiple in its full-court defensive scheme, an assistant coach should be put in charge of evaluating those different forms of defensive attacks. If a particular defense or stunt is more effective than another, the defensive team should ride that particular horse (until the opposition has corrected their problem). A precise, clear, and easy way to evaluate the performance level of each specific zone press and each individual stunt can be measured with the points (allowed) per possession form of evaluation. This statistic keeps track of how many times a particular defense is used (per quarter) and how the opposition has fared against it. Did the opposition turn the ball over? Did they survive the press but not score, or did they score as a direct result of the defensive alignment or stunt? The number of points that the defensive team scored as a direct result of their defense can also be recorded. This data allows the coaching staff to make informed and logical decisions during time-outs, quarter breaks, or at halftime. Coaches should keep statistics on each press defense that is used during the course of each game to see which one is the most efficient and successful and then let those statistics help determine which defense(s) to continue using or which defense to not use.

- Coaching staffs should develop their own specific "breakdown drills" for every phase of the defense. Breakdown drills teach and improve the fundamentals of the individual players and the team defense in a concentrated period of time.

- Coaches must make sure that some of these breakdown drills are transition drills both to get your team *into* the actual press defense and also *from* the press defense into your instant offense.

- Coaches should constantly analyze players' performances and inform each player of his individual defensive (as well as separate offensive grade) and award the players with the highest grades the most playing time.

- Techniques must be thoroughly taught, explained, and drilled for a team to be efficient in any or all of these full-court zone press defenses. Following are some of those necessary techniques that must be drilled upon daily to all players.

Full-Court Press Defense Techniques

- Defensive pressing players should remember T-I-P-S: (Proper) *Technique*, (Lots of) *Intensity*, (Proper) *Positioning* (on the court), (Proper) *Stances* by all five defenders, whether they are trapping, on the ball, or off the ball.

- Many half-court man-to-man defensive techniques should be used in the same manner or possibly slightly modified in the full-court zone press defensive scheme:
  ✓ The on-the-ball defender's stance and pressure on the opponent's ball handler can be very similar, especially in dictating the direction the ball handler should and should not go.
  ✓ The positioning of many off-ball zone press defenders can be very similar to half-court man-to-man defenders: The man-to-man defensive concept of maintaining a ball-you-man-in-your-zone-area is the same at full court as it is in half court.
  ✓ The stance of many off-ball zone press defenders can also be very similar. Defenders not on the ball are in a pistols stance both at half court and in full-court defenses.
  ✓ Zone press defenders who are aggressively denying the ball to an offensive player who starts in the middle of the zone press or has flashed to the middle of the zone press should have a stance that is similar to man-to-man post defense or perimeter denial defensive stances at the half court.
  ✓ The stance and positioning of defenders that are on the weakside of the zone press should be similar to man-to-man half-court defensive helpside defenders: ball-you-man flat triangle in a pistols stance.

- Full-court press defenses must always execute the proper full-court press techniques:
  ✓ All full-court press defenders must use the sideline, baseline, and 10-second timeline as extra defenders.
  ✓ When trapping the basketball, coaches should emphasize the trapping techniques by saying, "No lines, no splits!" When the ball is near a line that the offense cannot cross, one defender has full responsibility in preventing the ball handler from squirting past the trapper, while the other defender can never allow the ball handler from splitting the trap via dribble or pass.
  ✓ Zone press defenders that are trapping the ball should form an "L" with both feet of each trapper.

✓ Those zone press trappers should not reach in and try for a steal, but instead should cross-face and trace the ball. Trappers should try to force each escape pass to be a lob pass that takes extra time to reach its destination.

✓ All zone press trappers should leave a one-foot spacing between the ball and themselves. Trappers should not let the ball handler off the hook with a cheap reach-in foul.

✓ Zone press trappers and off-the-ball defenders should not watch the flight of the ball of any opponent's pass before reacting to the pass, but instead quickly sprint to where they anticipate the pass will land.

✓ All zone press defenders should always get to ball level, whether the ball is advanced via dribble or pass. Those defenders should sprint to get to the new ball level and look for opportunities to wolf the ball from behind.

✓ Zone press defenders that have an opposing dribbler approaching them should stalk the dribbler and never overcommit to the dribbler. Make the dribbler slow down as he tries to read the stalking defender. This technique gives the defense time for other defenders to get back to protect the basket as well as gives potential wolf defenders time to look to back tip the basketball as they wolf the dribbler and get to the new ball defender.

✓ Zone press defenders that become basket protectors or safeties should not gamble but maintain protection of their basket, prevent easy shots, and force the offense to make more passes to buy their teammates more time to get back to the basket.

Full-Court Press Defense

When using a multiple defense, a simple defensive numbering system is needed. A single digit represents only the half-court defense, while a double digit represents the full-court defense. The 1-2-1-1 or 1-2-2 full-court press is called the 1 press, and is represented by the number 1. It is the first of two digits. The 2-1-2 full-court press could be named the 2 press, and is represented by the number 2. It is the first of two digits. The 2-1-2 full-court press where the front line of the defense is face guarding and strongly denying the inbounds pass could be named the 3 press, and is represented by the number 3. It also is the first of the two digits.

Any half-court defense could possibly be combined with any press and utilized. These half-court defenses and their respective identification numbers could be the number 0 for a half-court match-up zone defense, the number 1 for the 1-2-2 half-court zone (or trap), the number 2 for the 2-3 zone, and the number 3 could identify the 1-3-1 zone (or trap.) The single digit number 5 could be used to name the half-court man-to-man defense.

Using this numbering system, a team could start in the 1 press and fall back into a 2-3 zone by simply calling out "12." To use the 3 press back into a half-court man-to-man, the number would simply change to 35. This makes for very easy and clear communication between players and coaches.

The 1 Press

The first discussion will be on the 1 press because this press can be used as a separate entity. It is usually the press used at the start of most games because it compels the offense into a 2-1-2 set.

The 1 press is a forceful and aggressive defense because it has an initial trap on the inbounds pass. You can also incorporate any of the stunts used in the other presses. With the various stunts, the 1 press can be used from the beginning of the game to the end.

Generally speaking, the tight wing is 02, probably the second-best ball defender. For discussion's sake, 02 will be designated as the tight wing. The tight wing (TW2) obviously aligns on the defense's left side of the court, since most opponents take the ball out-of-bounds on that particular side of the court (Diagram 4-1).

TW2 positions himself behind and on the inside of the offensive player in his area. This alignment is to prevent getting beaten vertically down the court as well as to the middle of the press. He wants to make sure the ball is passed to his side of the court

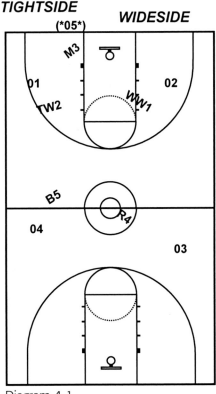

Diagram 4-1

and definitely in front of him. He can play a little softer than the wide wing. The wide wing would want to play tighter on his assignment because he wants to discourage the pass to the wideside. The line of least resistance is for the opposition to initially inbounds the ball on the tightside of the court.

Most likely, the wide wing (01), should probably be the best ball defender on the team. For discussion's sake, designate 01 as the wide wing and 02 as the tight wing.

The wide wing (WW1) aligns opposite of the tight wing, somewhat similar to the tight wing's overall defensive positioning in relationship to the man in his area. WW1 might want to play in a line between the inbounds passer and the player in his area, which would encourage the pass away from him and into the tightside of the court. This defender will have a much higher priority of denying the initial inbounded pass to the man in the wideside of the court by being in much more of a denial stance.

The defense should want the ball inbounded on the tightside to allow a double-team trap on the first pass. TW2 and M3 trap this first pass. The wide wing is most likely going to be protected from getting beaten on lob passes over his head because of constant pressure on the ball (by the Monster). The backboard, the rim, and the net also prevent semi-lob passes from the Trigger to the wideside. A much slower bounce pass would have to be used by the Trigger. This pass is the easiest to steal or deflect from a denial stance. The most effective defensive play is to have the opponents enter the ball on the tightside of the court. Try to encourage this by making this pass the line of least resistance, then trap and deny all advancing passes or dribbles. The only outlet is the reverse pass, and you want to encourage that pass (the line of least resistance).

The Bandit in the 1 press aligns in the second line of defense on the defense's left side of the court, generally just on the far side of the 10-second timeline within four to five feet from the sideline. The Bandit is the slower of the two post players, and in this discussion will be 05 and called B5.

The Robber also positions himself in the second line of defense on the defense's right side of the court, generally just on the far side of the 10-second timeline within five to six feet from his sideline. Most likely, the Robber is the quicker of the two post players, and in this discussion will be 04 and called R4.

In the 1 press, the Monster is the player who starts out defending the opposition's Trigger, so he would automatically be on the offense's tightside directly on the opponent's Trigger at the baseline. He will start in a cross-face stance to help discourage long throws and lob passes. He always traces the ball (he has his arms and hands on the same plane as the ball). This player must be very athletic, quick, and with good basketball instincts. For the discussion, the Monster will be the offense's small forward (03) and called M3.

Overall, the Monster (M3) should most likely be the defensive pressing team's best athlete and the best instinctive player. Obviously, he must possess good lateral speed and quickness. Ideally, his height and length can be contributors to his overall defensive prowess. Possibly the most important quality that the Monster (M3) must possess is that he has good basketball instincts and a high basketball IQ with a true nose for the ball.

If coaches want to give a slightly different look to their 1 press, they can tandem up the two backline defenders, R4 and B5. B5 would position himself near the center jump circle in the center of the floor, and R4 would line up vertically behind B5 as far back as the opponent's free throw line (Diagram 4-2).

Most offenses are right-handed, so most of the defense's tightsides are on their own left side. Because offensive Triggers stay out from under the basket, the tightside is an even smaller area to defend, compared to the wideside of the court. M3's first

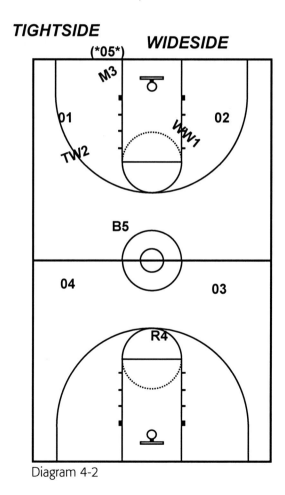

Diagram 4-2

responsibility is to prevent the quick, long throw to an opposing player streaking down the court (before the 1 press can be established). His second responsibility is to strongly discourage the inbounded pass to any opponent on the wideside of the court. His third responsibility is to prevent a lob pass to either side of the court.

The Monster cannot allow the ball to be flung or slung over the top of the 1 press or before the 1 press can be set up. The wide wing (WW1) can also put more denial pressure on the man in his area to encourage the inbounds pass to the tightside, thus allowing a better opportunity for a successful quick, hard trap on the ball (by M3 and TW2). The Bandit (B5) and the Robber (R4) must also help stop the quick, long throw by sprinting back to their initial positions and looking over their shoulder for a long pass as they retreat to form the backline of the press defense.

The Monster (M3) is the multi-dimensional player that aligns in various initial positions in each of the three different presses. If the defense is executing the 2 or the 3 press, the Monster (M3) starts in the center of the 2-1-2 defensive alignment, behind the first level of defense (TW2 and WW1) and in front of the last level of defenders (B5 and R4). The Monster (M3) starts in the middle of the court but slightly behind the backcourt's free throw line. M3 matches up with any offensive opponent located in the middle of the press. The other four defenders basically align themselves approximately in the same locations as they do in the 1 press (Diagram 4-3). Hence, the only defender who makes an adjustment from the 1 press to the 2 press is the Monster (M3). The other four defenders race to their positions regardless of the zone press that is called for as soon as their team has scored.

In the 3 press, (TW2) and (WW1) are in a total face-guarding stance. They aggressively attempt to completely deny any inbounded pass from the opposition's Trigger. The Monster (M3) now initially plays with more of a center field, stop the lob pass defensive position/location, stance, and mind-set. M3 should cheat over slightly to the side of the opponent's offensive inbounds passer (that will always be referred to as their Trigger). The 3 press's last level of the defenders, (B5) and (R4), basically align and play in the same initial locations/positions they start in with the 2 press. This simplicity and consistency of the alignments of almost every defender in all three full-court zone presses is still another advantage of using all three of the zone presses being discussed (Diagram 4-4).

For the 1 press, when the long throw is denied by the overall efforts of M3, B5, and R4, the ball is encouraged and channeled to be inbounded on the tightside (with the combined efforts of TW2 and WW1). The Monster (M3) and the tight wing (TW2) immediately form an L-trap on the ball with a no lines and no splits technique. Other key trapping techniques that must be stressed are the Monster (M3) and the tight wing (TW2) should cross-face and trace the ball. They should chest-bump the ball handler to apply maximum pressure on the ball handler. The defense also does not want to let the ball handler off the hook with a cheap foul.

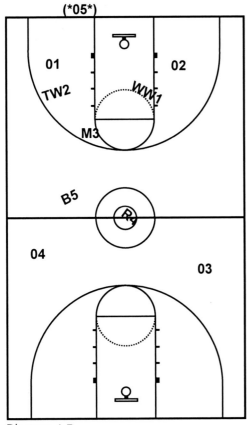

Diagram 4-3

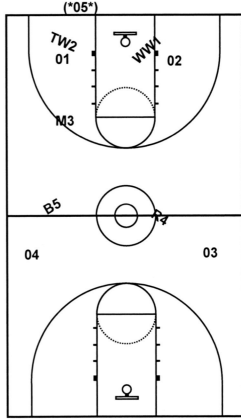

Diagram 4-4

On the inbounds pass, the wide wing (WW1) should jump to the ball and immediately sag off to protect the middle. The Bandit (B5) should protect the long sideline pass on the new ballside. The Robber (R4) should be in the proper position and stance to stop the long diagonal pass as well as protecting the basket as he now becomes the weakside backline defender. His rule is that no opponent can get behind him.

Proper spacing and proper stances and locations by all five defenders are extremely important (T-I-P-S). Each off-the-ball defender should always adhere to the philosophy and concepts of "the farther the man in his area is from the ball, the farther he can be from that man (in his area.)." Each of the four off-the-ball defenders should always be in a ball-you-man-in-your-zone-area location/position on the defensive court. Diagram 4-5 shows three of the four off-the-ball offensive players being completely covered. It displays a hard trap on the inbounds pass receiver. The only somewhat possible receiver left open, 02, is located in the ball reversal passing lane.

Once the ball is inbounded, many opposing offensive teams will try to attack the 1 press by ending up in a 2-1-2 offensive set to attack the gaps of the 1 press. This action falls right into what the defense actually wants the opposition to do. You will notice in Diagram 4-5, the line of least resistance is to reverse the ball to 02. When the offense reverses the basketball, the offense is in a 2-1-2 set, and the defense is matched, also in a 2-1-2 alignment (Diagram 4-6).

The slides of the 1 press have placed the defensive personnel in almost the identical 2-1-2 opponent's offensive spot-ups, when the ball is reversed from tightside to wideside. On the reversal pass, the Monster (M3) immediately jumps toward the pass and sags off to protect the middle as he slides to the same area that WW1 is originally defending. When M3 gets to the area to cover the offensive player that is posting up in the middle of the press (03), he then releases the wide wing (WW1) so that WW1 (as the new ball defender) can first close out on the ball (02) and then fan the ball down the sideline on the opposite side of the court. It must be constantly stressed to WW1 not to release protection of the middle area until M3 actually gets to that middle area to release WW1 to the new ball handler (02). Then, and only then, should WW1 close out with the proper fanning techniques on the new ball handler (on

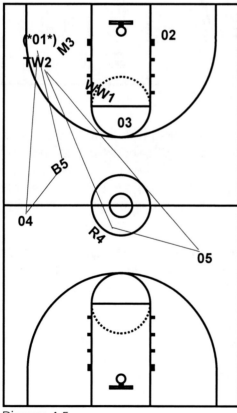

Diagram 4-5

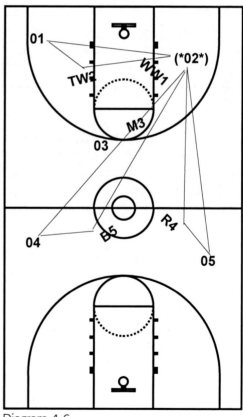

Diagram 4-6

the new ballside). The Bandit (B5), who is now on the new weakside, rotates back to protect the basket, while the Robber (R4) has positioned himself in a new ball-you-man-in-your-zone-area flat triangle on the new ballside. R4 is now ready to become the sideline trapper with the new ball defender WW1 should O2 advance the ball up the sideline. Diagram 4-6 displays the proper angles and the proper positioning of the players defending the advancing pass. Notice the line of least resistance is the ball reversal pass back to O1.

After the initial trap and the following escape reversal pass are completed, the 1 press takes on a different defensive approach than its original aggressive trapping philosophy. It now possesses more of the mind-set, attitude and characteristics of the 2 press.

After the initial hard trap on the tightside is followed by a reversal pass to the wideside, the offense has not actually advanced the ball (but has allowed the defensive team an excellent chance to double-team the ball while eating up part of the 10 seconds allotted in the backcourt). With the reversal pass, the 1 press becomes more of a waiting press that encourages the dribble to be made. Not only does the defense now encourage the opposition into dribbling the ball, but, more importantly, it now dictates where the dribbler must go. The defense takes on even more of an actor mentality and attitude, while making the opposition's offense into much more of a reactor mind-set. The dribble action will take more time than passing the ball and the 10 seconds allotted to the opponent's press offense is rapidly being expended.

This sudden and drastic new approach by the defense can somewhat shock the opposition into a different plan of action. The defense again becomes the actors and forces the opposition to again become the reactors. This shift forces the offensive team to make a decision on how to attack the press that has completely changed the atmosphere and the attitude of the defense. The offense must react and adjust to the defense by changing its approach and philosophy of trying to survive the new defensive press attack.

On the reversal pass out of the initial trap on the tightside, to the wideside, the new dribbler (O2) is encouraged, influenced, and forced to go down his sideline toward the timeline. These two lines serve as two additional defenders for the pressing team. The backline defender on the new ballside (R4) is there, also ready to trap the dribbler with WW1 (and its two additional defenders) near the sideline and on either side of the timeline. Either side of the 10-second line has its own advantages for setting the trap. The coaching staff can decide where they want the wideside dribble trap to be sprung, or they can leave it entirely up to the flow of the defense. Diagram 4-7 shows WW1 encouraging or fanning O2 to drive up the sideline. It also shows the location of the two deep defenders in relation to their receivers.

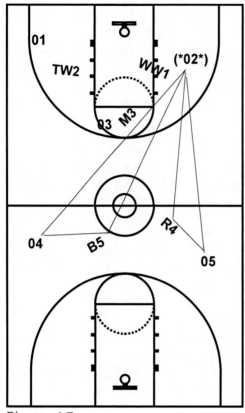

Diagram 4-7

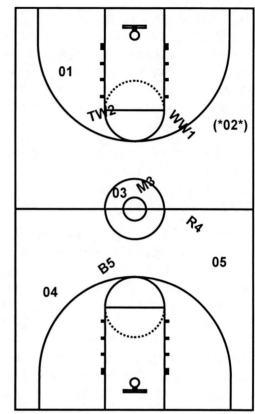

Diagram 4-8

After the initial double-team trap (tightside) opportunity is used with no turnovers resulting (and some of the 10 seconds is wasted), the only pass allowed would be to a player that is actually the farthest from the basket—a ball reversal. On ball reversal, the ball is fanned down the wide sideline, and the 1 press defensive spot-ups become identical to the opponent's offensive spot-ups. The 2-1-2 alignment of the defense exhibits TW2 and WW1 in the frontline, M3 protecting in the middle, and B5 and R4 in the backline. Diagram 4-8 displays 02's defensive positioning after advancing the ball halfway down the sideline. It also shows the proper positioning of the back two defenders in relation to their receivers.

As the ball is being advanced via the dribble, WW1 forces the ball down the sideline, and R4 bluffs and retreats before finally attacking the dribbler near the timeline and the sideline. TW2 drops to protect the middle, and M3 shoots the (diagonal) gap toward the new deep ballside corner, looking for a lob pass to intercept. Diagram 4-9 shows the trap being set just before the timeline. It shows M3 and TW2 shooting the gaps for possible interceptions. These two gaps are the natural passing lanes for 02. Diagram 4-9 also shows B5 retreating to protect the area of the basket.

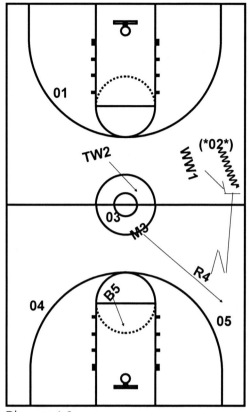

Diagram 4-9

This new ballside corner area is the area that should appear to the dribbler to be the open area as the sideline trap is about to be set. M3 has an excellent chance of intercepting a lob pass from 02 to 05 since he is out of the line of sight of the dribbler/passer (02). 02 has the double fear of getting trapped in a highly vulnerable area and the 10-second count violation being called. 02 will want to pass the ball quickly. Quickly means "hurried up," and hurried up to an offensive dribbler can oftentimes be translated to turnovers.

WW1 and R4 maximize their trapping skills along with M3 having even greater opportunities when all three defenders utilize the proper T-I-P-S. Again, trapping in either the backcourt or the frontcourt side of the timeline has different advantages. Regardless of which side of the time line the trap is going to be set, WW1 must narrow the dribbling alley of 02 as he approaches the timeline, which prevents the dribbler from splitting the trap. If the split of the trap does occur, both trappers (WW1 and R4) instantly sprint and wolf the ball as they both hurry to get to the (new) ball level. They run along beside the dribbler and look to back-tip the basketball as M3 attempts to stall and corral the dribbler. From there, with the offense only surviving (and not defeating) the 1 press, the defense can transition easily and quickly into its half-court defense.

The 2 Press

When a coaching staff elects to only play the 2 press, either the wide wing (WW1) and the Robber (R4) or the tight wing (TW2) and the Bandit (B5) make the sideline trap on their respective sides of the court (Diagram 4-10).

The better ball defenders (most likely the two guards) should be aligned in the first line of defense. The Bandit (B5) and the Robber (R4) align themselves in almost identical locations in the backline of the defense with R5 dropping deeper to protect the long throw. The most drastic change in positioning is to move the Monster (M3) from the very front of the 1 press to the very middle of the 2 press. There, the Monster (M3) can capitalize on his athletic skills, his instincts, and his nose for the ball to first protect and deny middle penetrating passes, and then to either shoot the gap and make interceptions after the defense has forced the dribble and ultimately forced sideline passes down either sideline.

When the ball is inbounded on the tightside against the 2 press, all defenders remain in the 2 press defensive spot-ups. The ball defender (TW2) fans the ball down the sideline with B5 (who is on the ballside sideline) bluffing and retreating as the ball handler dribbles down the sideline. When and if B5 attacks the dribbler is somewhat dependent upon how fast and how out-of-control the dribbler (O1 in this case) becomes as he dribbles down the sideline (Diagram 4-11).

M3 protects the middle lane of the press from any penetrating passes. As TW2 fans the ball down the sideline, the closer the dribbler approaches the timeline, the closer the spacing (dribble alley) between the dribbler (O1) and the ball defender (TW2) becomes. The ballside backline defender (B5) keeps the dribbler (O1) guessing on whether he will come up to trap the ball, or wait to trap the ball later or to never trap at all. The coaching staff's teaching/coaching points of emphasis are bluff (to trap) and retreat (back toward the deep sideline) and for B5 to dance back and forth to keep the dribbler guessing (Diagram 4-11).

If the ball continues down the sideline, TW2 applies more and more pressure on the dribbler, further narrowing the dribble alley, with B5 still bluffing and retreating. While still protecting the pass to the middle, M3 gets into position to diagonally shoot the gap toward the ballside deep corner. R4 becomes more and more prepared to drop to protect the basket. The weakside frontline defender (WW1) must quickly and efficiently perform his defensive slides and rotate to the middle of the press to replace M3 as the sole protector of the heart of the defensive press. Diagram 4-12 displays the 2 press out stunt trap being set in front of the 10-second timeline. It shows WW1 and M3 shooting the gap and R4 rotating back to protect the basket. R4 applies the concepts of the defender the farthest from the ball being able to defend both the basket as well as the man (in his area).

If the dribbler gets past the ball defender (TW2) and a possible trapper B5, TW2 and B5 must sprint and wolf the dribbler as other defenders (specifically M3) try to

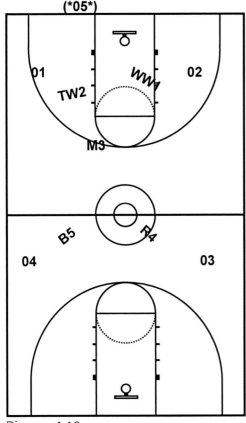

Diagram 4-10

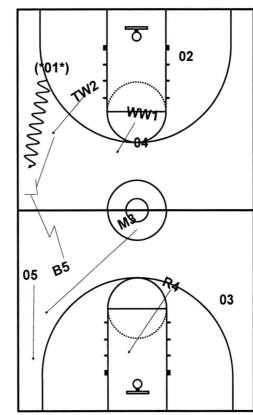

Diagram 4-11

slow and contain the dribbler. No easy shots or lay-ups must be surrendered. If lay-ups and easy shots are eliminated, the defense can press without fear of giving up easy points and allow the zone press (with its many attacking options) to operate a larger number of opportunities. The more opportunities a defensive team can press, the more potential turnovers can be produced from the press defense.

At the designated trapping spot, TW2 and B5 attack the dribbler. M3 shoots the gap toward the ballside deep corner, WW1 covers the middle passing lane, and R4 protects the basket. Depending upon whether the trap is in front or behind the timeline and where 02 is, WW1 continues to drop to the middle or steps back up to shoot the gap on a reversal escape pass, possibly to 02 (Diagram 4-12).

Diagram 4-13 shows the proper flat triangle positioning of the three off-the-ball defenders after the trap has been set by TW2 and B5. Notice how each defender is properly positioned to steal or deflect any lob pass. Again, the line of least resistance pass for the opposition's offense is the reversal pass to 02.

Some coaches may wonder why the weakside backline defender (R4 when the ball is dribbled down the defense's left or tightside of the court and B5 when the ball

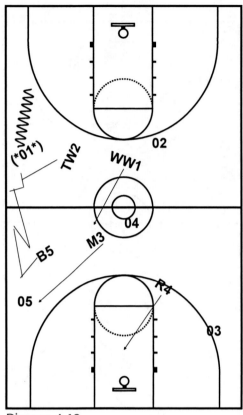

Diagram 4-12

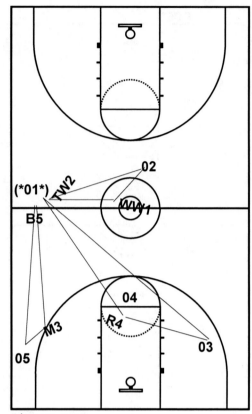

Diagram 4-13

is fanned down the defense's right side) isn't the defender that shoots the gap for the long sideline pass. That question is a valid one, to which several fundamentally sound answers can be provided. The only other defender that could possibly shoot the gap when the ball is dribbled down the defense's left sideline into the deep corner would be the weakside backline defender (either R4 from the left or tightside or B5 from the right or wideside). Our first reason is that there would then have to be a second person rotating to then become the basket protector (if the weakside basket protector of the 2 press was to become the sideline gap shooter and interceptor), and that person would have to be M3. That means M3 would have to first protect the middle and then rotate back to become the new basket protector. Both assignments of M3 are too vital for one of those assignments to not be completed successfully. The second reason is that either R4 or B5 would most likely be in the vision of the dribbler as the ball handler dribbles down the sideline, and fewer chances would be taken by the dribbler/passer if he were to see and anticipate the potential interception of the deep corner pass. Still another very important reason is that the designated Monster (M3) is going to be a much quicker and more intuitive defender (with a nose for the interception) than presumably the two biggest and slowest defenders (R4 and B5). Still a fourth credible reason is that the designated Monster has the same responsibilities for the long sideline pass on either side of the court, whereas you would have to have both B5 and R4 efficiently taught and trained to be those sideline hustlers to be the designated interceptors. Summarily, the Monster is by far the most capable and qualified defender to be the lone defender who will be looking to shoot the gap on sideline traps on either side of the court (Diagram 4-13).

As previously mentioned, trapping the ball in front of the 10-second line has specific disadvantages and advantages. One big disadvantage is that the entire court must continue to be defended, since the ball could be reversed to the opposite side of the court while still in the backcourt. The biggest advantage of trapping on the backcourt side of the timeline is that the offense only has 10 seconds for their offense in the backcourt, and most likely a good portion of the offense's 10-second time limit has been consumed even before the sideline trap is sprung. Running out of time may cause the offensive ball handler to panic and force some type of turnover.

A big advantage of trapping in the frontcourt is that the area that the defense must defend is reduced to just the frontcourt, but with the disadvantage being losing the 10-second time limit that the opposition erased after bringing the ball across the timeline. Decreasing the amount of court space the off-the-ball defenders must defend could outweigh the loss of the time limit restriction on the opposition's offense.

Regardless of where the trap is sprung, if the escape pass actually is successfully made out of the trap, all off-the-ball defenders must rotate and then relocate in the new proper ball-you-man-in-your-zone-area flat triangles while getting into the proper stances. The press is ready to retrap, search for turnovers, and shoot the gaps.

Diagram 4-14 displays the reversal pass to 02. TW2 jumps to the ball and quickly moves back to the center to help, releasing WW1 to cautiously close out on the ball to cover the new ball handler. M3 quickly moves to the center of the court, allowing TW2 to cover more to the opposite side of the ball. R4 rotates into the sideline passing lane, covering any player in that area, and B5 rotates to protect the side away from the ball and more importantly to protect the basket.

If the team is initially in the 2 press, and the ball is reversed to the original wideside, M3 immediately moves back more to the middle to release WW1 to close out on the ball that is now located on the wideside of the court. The new ball defender, who is now WW1 still fans the ball down his sideline but works in partnership with the Robber (R4), who is now bluffing and retreating toward the dribbler. The dribbler should be dribbling down the offense's left sideline. In addition to the other advantages of fanning the ball down the sideline; this opposing dribbler, who very well likely could be right-handed, must now have to use his weak hand to keep the ball out of the ball defender's reach as he is fanned down that sideline. This technique gives the defensive team still another possible defensive benefit that can and should be utilized. Eventually, WW1 and R4 should trap the ball somewhere near the timeline on either side of the timeline.

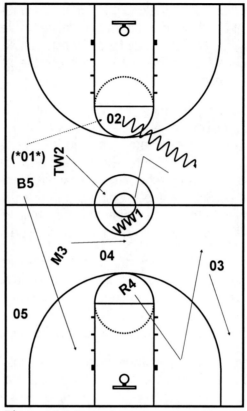

Diagram 4-14

WW1 and R4 should also utilize the same all-important trapping techniques (no lines/no splits and cross-face and trace the ball). With the ball on this side of the court, TW2 must sag off to protect the middle, with M3 again gets ready to shoot the gap (from a somewhat hidden location) to intercept the long sideline pass. B5 rotates back to protect the basket as the new defensive safety. TW2 would perform the significant task of protecting the middle of the defense while the two potential trappers (WW1 and R4) prepare to spring their trap on the dribbler (02) (Diagram 4-15).

If the ball continues down the sideline on the wideside of the court, WW1 applies an increasing amount of pressure on the dribbler and narrows the spacing between the ball and him (the dribble alley). R4 discourages the long sideline pass as he utilizes the bluffing and retreating techniques to confuse the dribbler (02) and maintains the proper ball-you-man-in-your-area flat triangle and the proper stance. If R4 feels that he cannot successfully surprise the dribbler and execute an effective trap, he can fake execution of the trap by bluffing his approach and remain defending the offensive opponent on that sideline to deny that pass. If not, WW1 and R4 set the trap on the offense's left side (or the defense's right side). The trap can be applied on either side of the 10-second line (with the same advantages and disadvantages as listed previously). On the defense's right side, M3 continues making his defensive slide toward the dribbler,

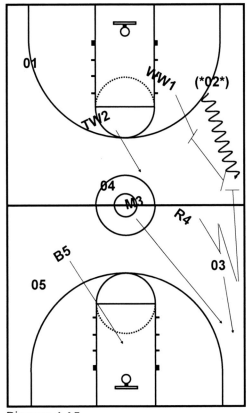

Diagram 4-15

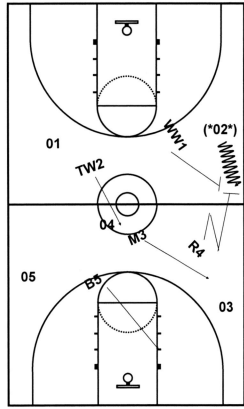

Diagram 4-16

and B5 rotates back to protect the basket. If the trap is set by WW1 and R4, M3 shoots the gap toward the deep ballside sideline. B5 must rotate to protect the basket with TW2 protecting the middle of the press (Diagram 4-16).

At the designated trapping spot (frontcourt or backcourt), with WW1 and R4 attacking the dribbler, the trap is applied with the same points of emphasis: no (side)lines and no splits (of the trap), tracing the ball, and cross-facing. Both players should avoid any cheap fouls. M3 shoots the gap toward the ballside deep corner while B5 protects the basket. Depending upon whether the trap is in front or behind the time-line and where 01 is located, TW2 continues to drop to the middle. If the ball is trapped in the frontcourt as shown in Diagram 4-17, then TW2 has a much smaller area to cover (since 50 percent of the actual court cannot be utilized by the offense). TW2 can therefore concentrate on a much smaller area of the court—the frontcourt. TW2 should then defend the middle of the press offense but still look for a possible interception on a pass back to 01. If the ball is trapped in the backcourt, TW2 must still physically protect the pass to 04 in the middle of the press, while mentally anticipating the reversal pass to 01 who has remained in the backcourt. TW2 is ready to shoot the gap (between 02 and 01) for the interception or deflection and potentially easy lay-up on the turnover. If 02 wilts under the pressure of the trap and turns his back on the

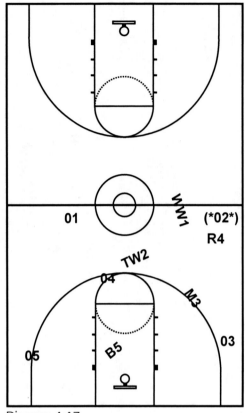

Diagram 4-17

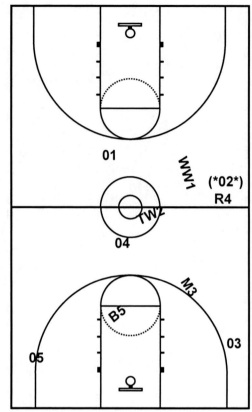

Diagram 4-18

defenders, TW2 can be even more aggressive, anticipate the reversal pass, and shoot the gap on the high reversal escape pass to 01. M3 shoots the gap down the long sideline on the dribbler's side of the court to possibly intercept the 02 to 03 pass in the new ballside deep corner). Diagram 4-17 shows the trap in the frontcourt. Diagram 4-18 displays the sideline trap by WW1 and R4 in the backcourt.

The 2-1-2 full-court zone press is somewhat of a hybrid of both the standard 1-2-1-1 full-court zone press and the traditional 2-2-1 zone press. The placement of defensive personnel in this press simply moves the Monster (M3) from the front (in the 1-2-1-1 press) or from the second line (in the 2-2-1 press) to the exact center of the zone press in the 2-1-2 press. The majority of the techniques, the positioning and the stances of defenders, and the slides of this combination press are almost identical for most defenders in this press as when either the 1-2-1-1 press or the 2-2-1 press is executed. This duplication of the majority of techniques for most defenders can only make all defenders' performances more efficient and ultimately more successful. It can also make the preparation time for these presses much less, while maintaining the execution levels needed for a high rate of success. Therefore, some practice time can then be devoted to other aspects of the game, while the opposition must devote more time to being ready to attack not one, but three seemingly different full-court zone presses.

The 3 Press

A third press has defensive personnel in the same general locations of the 2 press with the exception that TW2 and WW1 both shift their position so that they are in a complete denial and face-guarding stance and location on the two nearest inbound pass receivers. M3 plays in a floating centerfield location and with a stance to help take away the predominant pass that the inbound passer is forced to make—the lob pass to the one receiver that is closest to the passer. This seemingly completely different (cosmetically and attitude-wise) press can be called the 3 press. Similar to both the 2 press in its initial alignment and similar to the 1 press in its initial action and temperament, the 3 press, has no significance as to what side the ball is originally inbounded.

Diagram 4-19 shows the 3 press alignment. Notice it looks exactly like the 2 press alignment except for the face-guarding techniques of TW2 and WW1. M3 faces the opponent's Trigger and shades his positioning over closer to the Trigger's side and reads his eyes before instantly reacting to the attempted inbounds pass. This separate entity is actually just another very similar zone press with a slightly different cosmetic look, while having the same basic defensive stunts.

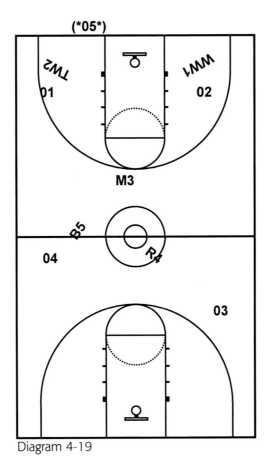

Diagram 4-19

If and when the ball can be inbounded without a turnover against the 3 press, all defenders immediately get into the 1 press defensive spot-ups with one major similarity and just one minor exception. Immediate double-team pressure is put on the first pass receiver, while the middle of the press and the basket are still both very much protected. The ballside sideline and reversal passes are also better defended. The one exception is that M3 has the freedom as a centerfielder to roam from sideline to sideline as he mirrors the opposition's inbounding Trigger, which means that he can and should trap the ball with one of his wing position teammates if and when the ball can be successfully inbounded. The other difference is that he will be the defender directly between the ball and the opposition's basket, while the wing defender trapping with him is the defender horizontally on the inside of the ball. If and when the ball is reversed out of the trap, M3 still is the only defender to jump to the ball and immediately drop to the middle of the press. If the ball escapes the trap via dribble, as always, both trappers sprint to get to the new ball level while looking to wolf the dribbler. The nearest off-ball defender that is sagging toward the middle would be the new designated stalker and container.

The entire different atmosphere that the 3 press initially brings can then attack the opposition's offense in a totally different and unique manner. Since the 1 press has a distinct difference in its approach to attacking the opposition's offense, mixing in the 1 press and the 2 press can force the opposition into confusion of how to successfully attack that specific press defense. When such drastic differences are found in the presses (with only minor cosmetic differences), the defense again has the advantage of time spent in preparation. Factor in the various stunts of the 3 press and the unpredictability of this press is exponentially magnified. Note that this press still requires the same proper T-I-P-S to be successful.

The 2-1-2 press is just a better overall defensive full-court press than the 2-2-1 press for several reasons. With the 2-1-2 press, the middle of the press is much more protected with M3 initially setting up in the middle. When most offenses see a zone press with a defender (M3) locked in the middle, most often press offenses don't even look to the middle for open pass receivers, let alone look to force a pass to the middle area.

The 2-1-2 press (the 2 press) has four stunts that can surprise the opposition's offense. The stunts vary as to when, where, and how the defense will attack the offense, and that is the main point of this press; it gives the defense opportunities for it to attack the offense instead of waiting to be attacked by the offense. In this press, not only can the trappers come from different locations and angles and surprise the dribblers, if they do come at all, but the gap-shooting interceptors also come from different locations and angles. In addition, the alignment of the 3 press can also allow the first pass to be surprise trapped. That alignment then gives an entirely different look to the press, making it much more unpredictable and therefore more difficult for an offense to counter, while still keeping the defense as simple as it originally was (Diagram 4-20).

Diagram 4-21 shows O1 receiving the pass in bounds from O5 and then O5 stepping inbounds. In the 2 press, the defense waits and does nothing until O1 begins his dribble. Remember that this waiting game is drastically different from the initial action of the 1 or 3 press, which can really distort the opposition's offensive plan. Also, it must be remembered that the 10-second time limit has already started while the opposition's offense must react to the defense's change and figure what to do next. Notice all attackers are covered correctly by the rule of the ball-you-man-in-your-area flat triangle.

Once the ball is inbounded, any of the 2 press's four defensive stunts may then be executed. These stunts can appropriately be called by these descriptive names: out, in, stay, and match. All can be utilized and all have the same basic three sets and initial appearances. All four stunts can surprise the opposition because the opposition will not be able to immediately read what stunt the defense is about to pounce on them (the four stunts will be offered in Chapter 5). Utilizing these four stunts and executing them in a variety of unpredictable ways will allow the defense to keep the opposition's offense off balance and out of rhythm. It has always been common knowledge that balance, rhythm, and self-confidence are necessary ingredients for an offense to be successful.

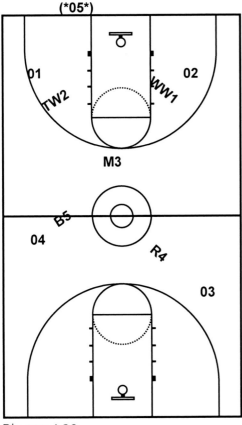

Diagram 4-20

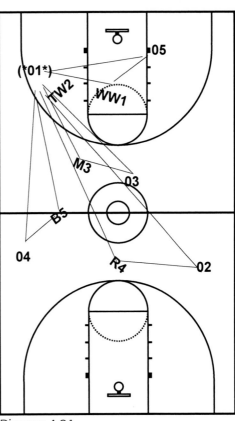

Diagram 4-21

Not recognizing the actual press the defensive team is utilizing means that the offensive team will not know the proper method to attack that defensive press. This lack of recognition gives the defensive team a tremendous advantage, and once the turnovers begin and the defensive spurts start, the turnovers and defensive success can become a landslide for the pressing defensive team and a confusing nightmare for the opposition's offense. Note that proper flat triangles and stances are also needed for defenders (in the 2 press or any of the three presses for that matter), even if the ball has not yet been inbounded (Diagram 4-22).

The 3 press can surprise the opposition with a high degree of denial pressure on inbounding the pass. This press with its particular alignment could be utilized particularly on a dead-ball situation, where the opposition's Trigger cannot run the baseline to inbound the ball, or after made free throws (where a slight lull in the action occurs). Each of these situations is an outstanding time to surprise the opposition as well as an ideal time for the pressing team to substitute players possibly more suitable to success for this type of zone press attack. If no turnovers occur off of the surprise and aggressive denial with the 3 press, then any of the 3 press's stunts (that are identical to the 2 press's four stunts) could then be applied after this change and surprise (defensive) set.

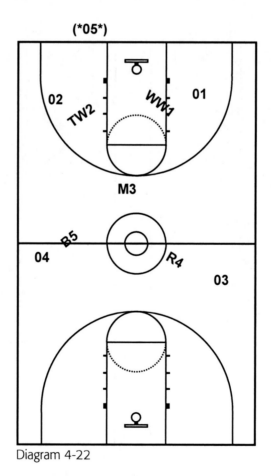

Diagram 4-22

These defensive stunts could be compared to offensive plays out of an offensive alignment/set. If no turnovers take place, any of the four basic 1, 2, or 3 press slides could then take place. This approach is similar to offensive continuities that maintain a constant attack on the defense. The multiple stunt factor makes the 3 press an even more aggressive and complex (to the opposition) press defense that will be difficult for the opposition's offense to predict, figure out, and solve. Diagram 4-23 displays the proper positioning of all defenders when the 3 press begins. Both frontline defenders, TW2 and WW1 face-guard their opponents to aggressively deny the inbounds pass to the opposition's probable best ball handlers. Notice, WW1 defends his man in his area with a slightly different body positioning. Also, M3 plays centerfield and acts as a helpside defender, particularly for TW2 to discourage lob passes from 04 to 02.

Diagram 4-24 illustrates action by the opposition if the ball is successfully inbounded with the ball being lobbed over the face-guarding TW2. As the lob pass is still in the air, the Monster (M3) should be able to react to the pass for any one of several possible turnovers (a fumble, bad pass, charge, travel). If no turnovers take place, M3 can trap the ball with TW2. WW1 would then sag off to the middle, while B5 plays the deep

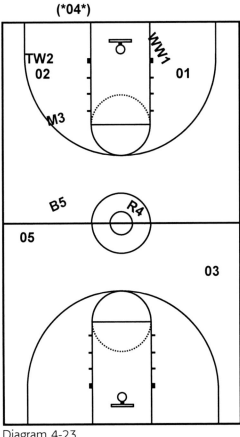

Diagram 4-23

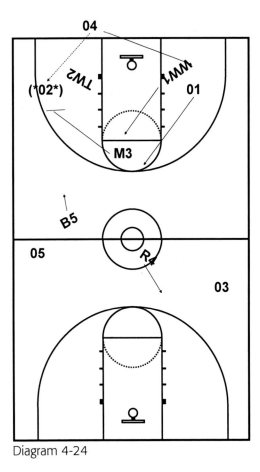

Diagram 4-24

ballside vertical pass and R4 protects the basket as they both would if the press were the 1 press.

The 3 press appears to be executed the same way the 1 press is executed when the ball is made to the tightside. This execution makes these two presses now even more similar in concept, and then much easier to teach. Yet the opposition perceives this defensive scheme to be just of the many aggressive, confusing, and complex presses. This confusion becomes still another great advantage gained by the defense.

If the ball escapes out of the initial trap set by TW2 and M3 (on the inbounds pass) and the ball is reversed to the wideside of the court, the defensive personnel should execute the same 1 press defensive slides and rotations versus wideside ball reversals. Defenders should end up in the exact locations as when the ball is reversed to the wideside versus the 1 press. That means that WW1 stays in the middle until M3 jumps to the ball, and then releases WW1 to cover the new ball handler. M3 would now have the middle. That rotation then allows WW1 to slowly and carefully close out on 01 who has just received the escape pass from 02 (Diagram 4-25).

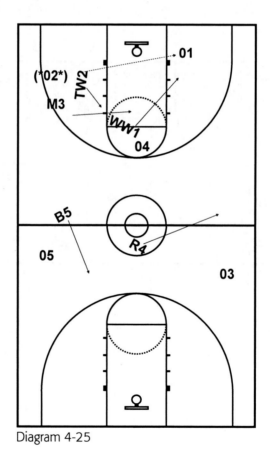

Diagram 4-25

The defensive team has tried to force turnovers with the face-guarding action before the ball is even inbounded and then follows this possibly surprise tactic with a quick trap (by TW2 and M3). If the ball can be escaped out of the trap on a ball reversal pass, the defensive team again rotates into a 2-1-2 defensive alignment that oftentimes has actually matched up to the opponent's current offensive alignment. From there, the similar techniques of the sideline trap near the timeline can be executed—on either side of the timeline. After the ball is reversed, the full-court zone press defense remains harassing the opposition's offense. The analogy of this part of the press could be similar to a half-court offense's continuity attack—after an offensive play is executed without producing points, the continuity offense remains in attack mode, so the zone press stunt continues its attack with its own version of a continuity (defensive) attack.

Diagram 4-25 shows the reversal pass to O1. M3 slides back to cover the middle and releases WW1 to go to cover O2. TW2 also races back to the middle to help out until he can recover to cover the left sideline. R4 moves into the passing lane down the right sideline, while B5 retreats to cover the basket area.

Some offensive opponents may initiate their press offense with a 4 across alignment. The defense can align itself in the 3 press (defensive set) and encourage the first pass to be made to the offensive player closest to the sideline (on either side of the court, protecting the middle of the press). Because of the initial denial press, sometimes opponents feel they must change and place their best passer as their Trigger just so they can safely inbound the ball. So the 3 press has immediately succeeded in forcing the opposition into possibly reacting to the press and making changes they are forced to make. These changes might not be the opposition's actual strengths and favorite things to do, but are forced to do so. The opposition may feel they must then reposition offensive personnel so that O5 and O4 are on the outside of the horizontal alignment, with O2 and O3 in the middle two positions. With the ball being denied to the middle of the press and passed to one of the two offensive players nearest the sideline, this shift may place the ball in the possession of a much inferior ball handler such as O4 or O5. The 3 press's new ball defender (TW2 on the defense's left and WW1 on the right) can again influence the dribbler (O5 or O4) to be fanned down the sideline so that any of the stunts could then be executed (Diagrams 4-26 and 4-27).

Diagram 4-26 shows the two better ball handlers on the inside of the four-across alignment being covered by TW2 and WW1. This coverage encourages the offense to pass to the sidelines, which is where the inferior ball handlers are located. Diagram 4-27 displays the ball being inbounded to the opposition where they have placed their possibly second-best ball handler (O2) and the subsequent rotations of the defense into the 2-1-2 set. The defense is ready to run one of its stunts that are the same as the other two zone presses discussed. As in the other two zone presses, any of the four stunts could be utilized that will highlight individual zone press defender's outstanding athletic abilities, skills, and talents, while also probing for individual or overall team weak links of the opposition's offense. Then other stunts might be used to more appropriately attack and take advantage of those discovered offensive weaknesses.

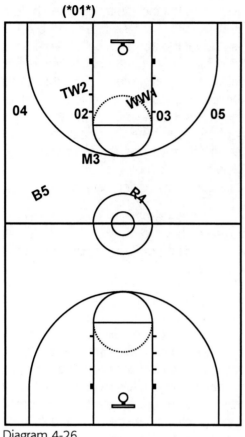

Diagram 4-26

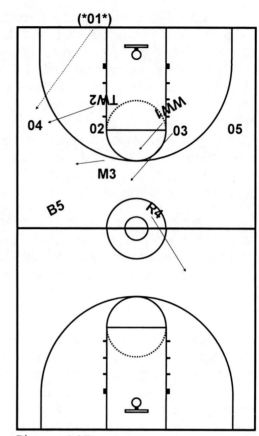

Diagram 4-27

Coaches should remember again that the mental capabilities of all individual defenders should be considered as well as the overall physical capabilities and talents. One particular team may have the skills to be able to have an expanded full-court defensive package, while another team may have a very limited full-court pressure defensive scheme. A team may have the physical skills and talents but might be limited mentally as to how many of the presses they can successfully use and how many of the stunts they could use in their defensive press package. A very important evaluation and decision must be made by the staff not to overextend its defensive package at the risk of being unproductive. But if a coaching staff believes that the mental and physical skills are present on that particular team, that defensive team should have the defensive firepower and explosiveness that could make a good basketball team a great team.

It should also be remembered that the three different defensive packages as well as the stunts can be added in small increments in a progressive manner as the season goes along and as the defensive players improve and progress.

The 1, 2, and 3 Press Stunts

This chapter deals with stunts that can be used when the defensive team is in position to execute any of the three presses. These stunts are not restricted to just these two presses. If the defensive team chooses to execute the 1 press in a typical manner (where the opposition initiates their offense with a pass to the defense's tightside, gets trapped, and then reverses the ball to the wideside), the defense is in the defensive spot-ups of either the 2 press or the 3 press. Any of the four stunts that will be discussed could be integrated within the actual 1 press, which could also happen if the ball was initially inbounded to the wideside.

For the sake of discussion, this chapter will discuss the first of the four basic defensive stunts being executed out of the 2 press. This first diagram will show that the ball is inbounded to the defense's tightside of the court, which places the ball on the defense's left side of the court.

This first stunt is appropriately called the out stunt. Once the ball is inbounded, immediate pressure is placed on the ball handler. TW2 pressures the ball to discourage passes and to encourage the dribble. Once the dribble begins, TW2 should then attempt to fan the dribbler down the sideline on his side of the court. B5 (who is now the third line defender on the ballside) should look to deny the long pass down his sideline, while being ready to work with TW2 to trap the ball near the sideline in front of the 10-second timeline. Every dribble made down the sideline should cause TW2 to increase the pressure on the dribbler and to decrease the spacing between the ball and himself. B5 is in the proper ball-you-man-in-your-zone-area flat triangle location as he discourages the long vertical pass with his bluff and retreat techniques before eventually springing the trap with TW1. The Monster (M3), in the center of the press, will initially protect the middle before looking to diagonally shoot the gap should a long sideline pass be attempted. WW1 (now on the helpside frontline) looks to drop to the middle of the press as the trap is about to be set. R4 (the helpside third line defender) should rotate diagonally down and over to protect the basket (Diagram 5-1). Diagram 5-2 illustrates the same 2 press out stunt, involving the same two trappers, but with the trap being sprung just across the 10-second line in the frontcourt. Many advantages exist when executing the out stunt in the frontcourt such as half of the court not having to be defended (Diagram 5-2). Diagram 5-1 depicts the out stunt using the trap in backcourt. Diagram 5-2 shows the same out stunt with the trap taking place in the frontcourt.

The objectives of the original 2 press ball defender (in this case, TW2) are to not only attempt to force the dribbler down the sideline, but to encourage him to speed up so that he will be an out-of-control dribbler when he eventually is trapped. If the dribbler slows down to stay under control, that can also make it even easier for TW2 to catch up and/or stay ahead of the dribbler. This technique makes it much easier to be able to contain and control the dribbler into the trap.

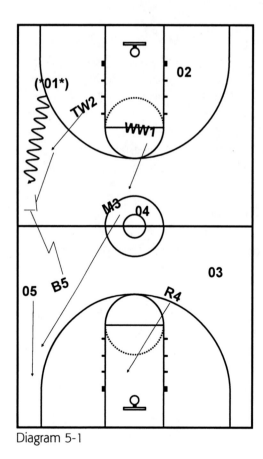

Diagram 5-1

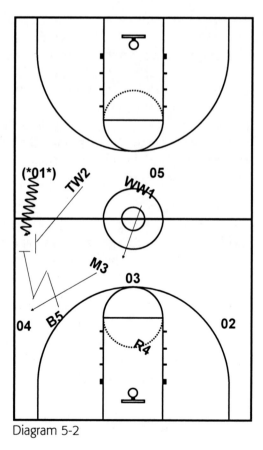

Diagram 5-2

Regardless of what the offense does, this press defense package has an answer and a countermeasure to attack the offense. If the dribbler dribbles fast and out of control down the sideline, the 2 press out stunt can be very effective with a hard trap near the sideline and timeline. If the dribbler elects to pass the ball down the sideline before the trap occurs, M3 has an excellent opportunity to intercept the pass. If the dribbler attempts to force the pass to the middle of the press, either M3 or WW1 should have a great opportunity of intercepting or at least deflecting the penetrating passes to the middle of the press. R4 should easily intercept the long diagonal crosscourt pass if he is in the correct location and stance and the proper amount of ball pressure is on the dribbler/passer. All off-the-ball defenders should be in the appropriate pistols stances and also in the proper ball-you-man-in-your-area flat triangles (similar to half-court man-to-man defensive philosophies and concepts). T-I-P-S, again, is a key technique for the successful execution of this press (Diagram 5-3).

If the ball initially is inbounded to 02, then the ball starts on the original wideside (that is, the ball starts on the defense's right side or starts on the offense's left side and the ball could then be reversed to the opposite side). Diagram 5-4 depicts the proper positioning of the off-the-ball defenders (using the flat triangle positioning techniques) with the ball before the ball is reversed to the original tightside.

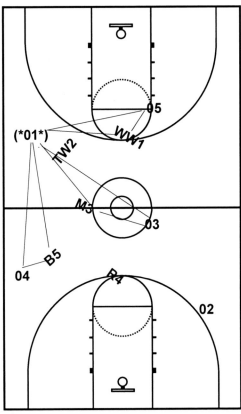

Diagram 5-3

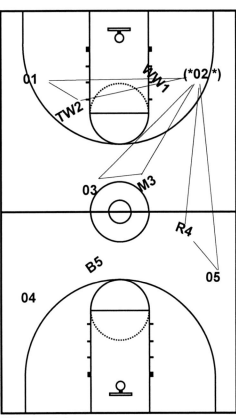

Diagram 5-4

With 02 having received the reversal pass, WW1 fans the dribble down the sideline. Every step that 02 dribbles the ball down the sideline, WW1 narrows the gap between the ball and himself. R4 denies the long vertical pass as he continues his bluff and retreat movement toward the dribbler. R4 eventually prepares to step up to trap with WW1. M3 prepares to shoot the gap to look to intercept the long deep sideline pass that appears to be open once R4 rushes up the sideline to trap the ball with WW1. The off-the-ball wing defender, TW2, is ready to drop to the middle, and B5 rotates over to protect the basket (Diagram 5-5).

If that sideline pass is completed and M3 rushes past the ball, M3 should reverse his direction and sprint and wolf the dribbler while R4, TW2, and WW1 try to also sprint and wolf the ball from behind. B5 stalks and tries to contain the dribbler and buy his teammates time to get back. Individual defenders will achieve more success if they use the appropriate T-I-P-S, including the ball-you-man-in-your-area flat triangles.

When the dribbler (on the wideside of the court) gets to the designated trapping area, R4 steps up to trap with WW1 near the sideline and also near the timeline. If the dribbler does not know when or where the trap will take place, the trap could very well surprise the dribbler. The same trapping techniques should be used to look for the various types of possible turnovers that could take place out of the trap, such as

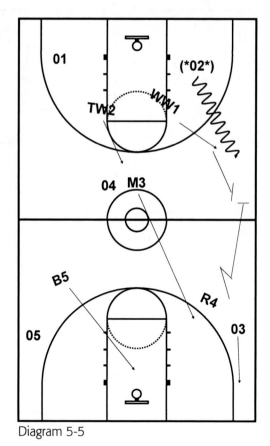

Diagram 5-5

offensive fouls, traveling, over and back violations, bad passes, fumbles, and such. M3 shoots the gap to look to intercept the long deep sideline pass (from 02 to 03). This pass appears to be open because M3 is out of 02's view. TW2 sags to the middle, and B5 rotates to protect the basket (Diagram 5-5).

Depending upon which side of the timeline the trap occurs, TW2 will decide how, when and where to play in the middle. Another factor on how all off-the-ball defenders position themselves is if and when the dribbler turns his back on the defensive pressure. If 02 faces a potential receiver, the defender in that area will be more aggressive for the anticipated interception.

A complementary stunt to the out stunt is appropriately called the in stunt. This stunt can neutralize how the opposing offense reacts to the press. It is a counter to the out stunt. By changing defensive stunts, the pressing defensive team can again be the actors and force the opposition's offense to have to be the reactors. This approach goes against the grain of most basketball games, where defenses normally must read and react to the offense's initial action. With multiple stunts, the offense must slow down to try to read, identify, and then react to the defensive stunt. Slowing down an offense allows the defense to be that much more effective and successful. The offense is becoming defensive and more passive, and the defense can become more aggressive and more of the attacking team. The offense is prone to get caught up in a defensive spurt—a series of opponent's possessions where there is a sudden explosion of various turnovers.

As the ball is being fanned down the sideline and the offense anticipates the sideline trap, the dribbler may elect to slow down and stay under control (to prevent various types of offensive turnovers). This offensive countermeasure may work against the traditional 2-2-1 full-court zone press or the 2 or the 3 press's out stunt, but it also plays right into the defense's hands when the defensive team is utilizing the in stunt. With the ball being on the tightside of the court and 02 having the ball and being fanned by TW2, the defensive stunt initially appears to be the out stunt. If the out stunt has been run a few times in succession, the in stunt becomes even more effective.

When 02 slows down his dribble to attempt to not get trapped down the sideline, TW2 (who initially is fanning the ball) can more easily run ahead of the dribbler to encourage a change of direction of the dribbler away from the sideline. The dribbler could very well employ a spin dribble away from the defender who is jumping ahead of him. This spin dribble would carry the dribbler toward the middle of the court. When the dribbler reverses the ball back to the middle away from TW2 cutting his dribble off, M3 should then surprise-attack the dribbler (from the dribbler's blind side). B5 bluffs and retreats on the original ballside sideline as he usually does in the out stunt, but with the in stunt, B5 never actually steps up to trap the dribbler, but stays and denies the vertical sideline pass. WW1 eventually sags inside to protect the middle when he sees M3 leaving the middle of the press to trap the ball (from the middle). R4 looks for the long, diagonal skip pass and still protects the basket (Diagram 5-6).

If the dribbler gets loose and splits the trap, R4 gets into the lane and protects the fort, does not surrender any easy baskets, and buys the defense time for his teammates to get back to help. All other defenders either sprint to get to ball level as they wolf the dribbler or if the defender is ahead of the dribbler, that defender must stalk the dribbler and slow him down.

If the offensive ball handler (O2) somehow does not commit a turnover from the surprise trap from the in stunt and somehow can make a ball-reversal pass, all five defenders should again jump to the ball (as all five defenders are to do after any pass is made against the press). On the ball reversal from O2 to O1, WW1 waits until M3 can slide back toward the middle, and then M3 releases WW1. WW1 then closes out on the new ball handler. He then fans the ball down the opposite (wide) sideline and the defensive attack continues with its continuity defense action: the out stunt (Diagram 5-7).

The basic actions of the out or in stunts are again in play. R4 (now on the new ballside) should bluff and retreat the dribbler to help trap the ball on the sideline with the new ball defender, WW1 if the out stunt is called. In the defensive press scheme,

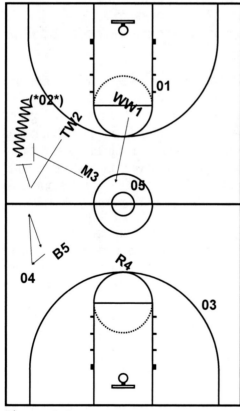

Diagram 5-6

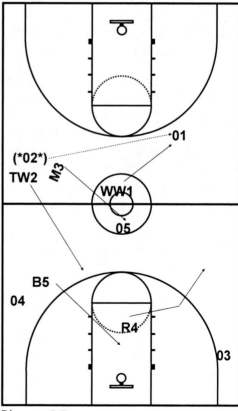

Diagram 5-7

if the defensive play (the in stunt) does not produce turnovers or points, call the out stunt on the other side of the court when the ball is reversed as your continuity stunt.

The bluff and retreat action executed by R4 will keep 01 off balance and to make the offense passive and less aggressive in its attack. With hard pressure always on the ball and forcing the dribble, if the long sideline pass is attempted, R4 is in position to intercept that long sideline pass. R4's positioning should discourage this long, dangerous pass. If 01 retains the dribble down the sideline, R4 could and should rotate up to trap the dribbler with WW1. M3 is centered up in the press protecting penetrating passes in the middle and basically hidden from the dribbler's vision. M3 again shoots the gap for the long sideline pass when R4 traps the dribbler near the sideline and timeline. As the trap is sprung, B5 rotates over from the new weakside to protect the basket. TW2 is ready to sag off to the middle of the press when M3 makes his diagonal move toward the new ballside sideline area (Diagram 5-8).

It must be stressed that the ultimate decision of the surprise jump trap of the ball handler can be made only by the ballside backline defender (B5 or R4). If doubt or hesitation is present, no out stunt should be executed. Instead, the original ball defender

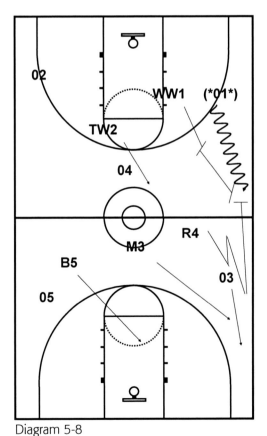

Diagram 5-8

(TW2 or WW1) should maintain the fanning of the basketball into the frontcourt, where the designated half-court defense will begin. No trap is set, but the offense not only has failed to score, but still has the ball in a location that is not dangerous to the defense, and the offense is probably wondering why there was no trap—*this* time. Will the trap be sprung the next time? Again, the defense has gained an advantage for the next possession with the unpredictability of these presses.

Diagram 5-8 shows WW1 and R4 using the timeline and the sideline to trap 01 with the ball still in the backcourt. After the in stunt and the reversal of the ball, the 10-second count is almost up, and the out stunt with the ball is still in backcourt. It is easy to see why the offense would panic.

If WW1 continues to fan the ball down the (wideside) sideline and across the time line, R4 now should continue his bluff and retreat techniques on 01. Another huge advantage the defense has is that the ball handler's 10-second time limit in the backcourt should quickly be running out. If the dribbler speeds up his dribble to beat the time limit and becomes an out-of-control dribbler, R4 has a better opportunity to force a turnover when he traps with WW1. This trap actually becomes the out stunt. Diagram 5-8 shows the trap occurring before the timeline. Diagram 5-9 displays the trap occurring after the dribbler crosses the timeline after the initial ball reversal.

This out stunt press action always takes place after any initial stunt (in or out) where the offense has successful completed a ball reversal. M3 shoots the gap (between the ball handler and the pass receiver) to defend 03 down the corner area near the sideline, while TW2 drops to protect the middle. B5 rotates back (from the current weakside) to again protect the basket. The degree that TW1 drops to the middle (when M3 shoots the gap) is also dependent upon whether 01 crosses the timeline or not. If the dribbler crosses the timeline, TW1 can drop farther toward the middle, because the amount of the court that the defense must defend is considerably smaller.

The offense might occasionally escape the in stunt by the dribbler splitting the trap. Drilling on this situation allows it to happen infrequently, but this seemingly offensive victory can very quickly and easily become a disaster for a ball handler and his teammates.

Consider such a situation: The in stunt is called and the ball begins on the defense's left side (Diagram 5-10). After TW2 influences the dribbler down the sideline until he then sprints ahead of 02 to cut him off and M3 then jump traps the ball, a defensive breakdown of some sort occurs. The ball handler (02) splits the trap that is to be set by TW2 and M3.

In this situation, all the players that are behind the ball should sprint and wolf to get to the new ball level. All defenders that are in front of the ball such as WW1, M3, and R4 should protect the basket and/or stalk and try to contain the dribbler. TW2 and M3 hustle to the new ball level by finding the angle of pursuit and sprinting back to

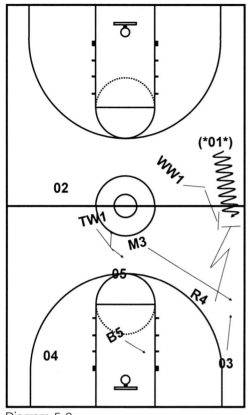

Diagram 5-9

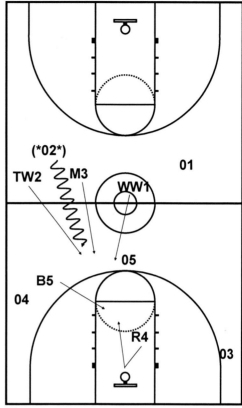

Diagram 5-10

get ahead of the ball. As they are sprinting back to the new ball level, they are trying to back-tip the dribbler from behind in the sprint and wolf technique. The dribbler is in a precarious position as he is facing three defenders in front of him and he also cannot see the two defenders attacking him from behind. The offensive advantage that the dribbler thought he had can become a nightmare and result in many types of turnovers that can quickly and easily be converted to scores by the hustling defensive team.

A third stunt of the 3 press is called the stay stunt. This stunt is an extension of the out stunt. It will be described with the ball being on the wideside of the court. Just like the in stunt, every defender's techniques and positioning of the stay stunt are exactly the same as the out stunt. The only difference is that the ballside backline defender (R4, in this case) bluffs and retreats but never fully rotates up to actually trap the ball. Instead, R4 must *stay* on his sideline area and looks for the interception from 01 to 03. WW1 must defend the ball using the sideline and timeline as extra defenders (instead of using R4.) In the stay stunt, the defense does not want to trap 01 and would like 01 to reverse the ball to someone who is a poorer ball handler on the opposite sideline (such as 02). The defense is playing away from the offense's individual strengths and hopefully capitalizing on offensive weaknesses that exists somewhere else (Diagram 5-11).

It is also possible to use the in stunt techniques without M3 coming over to trap. This strategy is particularly sound when WW1 can force 01 to reverse dribble but still keep 01 under control. Usually, 01 will reverse and pick up his dribble, especially after the in stunt has been executed a few times. If the dribble is picked up, the 10-second time limit becomes an even more likely type of opponent's turnover as could intercepted passes (Diagram 5-11).

The stay stunt is used especially if the offensive opponent uses one of their post players (who generally are not good dribblers or passers) as their offensive Trigger. Diagram 5-12 shows the Trigger (05) inbounding the ball to the tightside of the court before then stepping inbounds as a potential pass receiver. 02 has cut through the heart of the defense into the frontcourt. This strategy is frequently used as a press breaker.

The stay stunt has the original ballside backline defender (B5 in this case) stay if and when the ball is fanned down the sideline. B5 does not rotate up to trap the ball with the ball defender (in this case, TW2). The pressing defense may want to influence the opposition to make a reverse pass from most likely one of their better ball handlers (01) to one of their worst ball handlers (05). The defense has gained

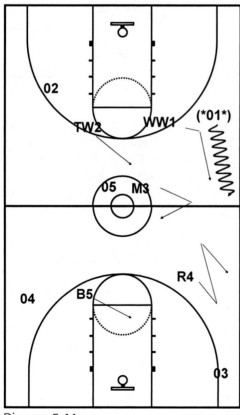

Diagram 5-11

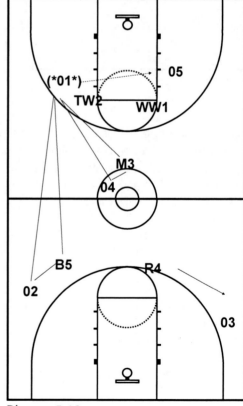

Diagram 5-12

a huge defensive personnel advantage by looking to take advantage of a discovered offensive weakness—05's poor ballhandling skills (Diagram 5-12).

If the defense then forces or influences the ball from the offense's right side to their left side with a poor ball handler who must use his weaker left hand (assuming that 05 is a right-handed ball handler), the defense has then gained an additional advantage. A second advantage for the pressing team is that the defensive personnel on that side of the court should be even stronger than on the tightside of the court. With the ball being inbounded and then reversed into the hands of one of the opposition's presumably worst ball handlers, the offense's backcourt 10-second limit could almost be ready to expire, still another advantage the defense can capitalize on. Once the ball is reversed to the wideside, the basic out stunt (the press defense's continuity action) should again be executed. Remember, the out stunt can be designated the defense's continuity attacking action that is always used after a reverse pass is made from an initially called stunt, which is one of the basic tenets of the full-court zone press defensive package. Should 05 be forced into a dribble down the sideline, WW1 and R4 will set the trap in the out stunt. Hopefully, this trap will occur in the backcourt with the 10-second rule providing a high level of panic.

The fourth stunt is called match and should be used when the offense attempts to counter the other three stunts. One way the offense could try to attack the press is by aligning their personnel in a diamond-shaped formation after the ball is inbounded. One possible defensive countermeasure can then take advantage of this type of offensive press attack by utilizing the match stunt. If the press offense overloads the zone press defense with more offensive players in a particular area, the defense should only give up the pass that would be the least damaging to the defense.

Diagram 5-13 shows the defense being in the 2 press and the ball being inbounded from 04 to 01. 04 steps inbounds and becomes the obvious pass receiver. That next pass would be a reversal pass back to 04, who is furthest from the opposition's offensive basket as well as most likely one of the offense's poorer ball handlers. R4 (who has no one in his area in this case) then rotates up to take 05 in the middle of the press, which frees up M3, who can then close out on the ball. This two-man rotation would then allow WW1 to match up to the offensive player in the wide wing area (in this case, 02). These chain reactions for these defensive rotations will take some time, but TW2 and WW1 both protect middle penetration while M3 waits until R4 releases him to then close out to the new ball handler. Keep in mind that the 10-second time limit on the offense is still ticking and there is actually no dribbling area for the new ball handler to utilize. TW2 and WW1 each cover an offensive wing. M3 remains in the middle to protect the middle post area until R4 releases him. Also, remember that this is a new look for the opposition to decipher and attempt to figure out. It may take the offense a few seconds to evaluate the new situation. From there, every defender has a specific man to guard and the full-court zone press basically switches to become a full-court man-to-man press—and the clock is ticking.

The match stunt could also be utilized when the offense tries to keep advancing the ball via a sideline dribble before reversing the ball and then continuing the same process. The match stunt is put into effect when the ball is reversed. This time, however, the ball is further down the floor. This stunt in the zone press defensive package makes the offensive counters to the regular stunts obsolete. The offensive advantages are turned into defensive countermoves, another advantage for the defense.

The offense has now burned some of its 10 seconds, especially when the ball is reversed after the dribble down the sideline, and the offense has to unexpectedly face a man-to-man defense, as well as the offense having a poorer dribbler with the ball. The better ball handlers (01 and/or 02) could possibly even be denied getting the ball back into their hands to force the weaker ball handlers to advance the ball down the court. The defense can attack the offense's weaker points and still have the time limit advantage and a change in the overall defensive scheme (Diagram 5-14).

The second method the 2 press defense can use to counter this passive type of offensive attack is shown on the first reversal pass (Diagram 5-15). When 04 receives the return pass from 01, TW2 and WW1 both center back up toward the middle only

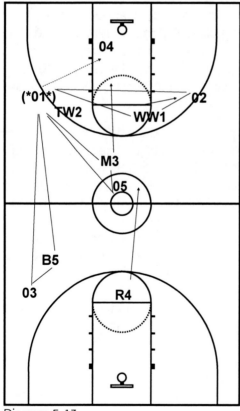

Diagram 5-13

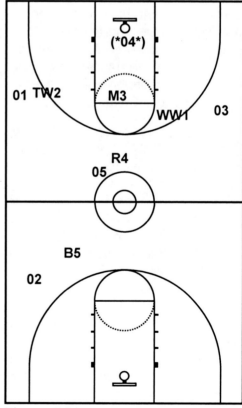

Diagram 5-14

slightly and stay slightly wider to discourage a new sideline pass and to encourage a gap dribble. The 10-second time limit only benefits the defense and the press defense can play a waiting game, while 04 (most likely, a poor ball handler) must make the decision on whether to attempt to make a (more dangerous) pass toward either sideline or to dribble into the perceived gap in the middle of the court.

Keep in mind the defense is now very likely attacking a major weakness in this press offense attack—having the ball in a poor and inexperienced ball handler's hands, (04), in the deep backcourt with the time limit again becoming a major factor. This situation compels the offense into making a hurried up decision, which could lead to many different types of offensive turnovers.

If the offense does elect to try to gap dribble into the teeth of the press, a predesignated wing defender (TW2 or WW1) can step further into the gap to be the sole defender. This new wing defender takes the dribbler while his teammate starts to step out to his respective wing area. With the dribble stopped, only the kick-out pass remains for the ball handler. Either wing should then be able to anticipate the pass to the sideline and then be able to fan the ball down their sideline and the continuity of

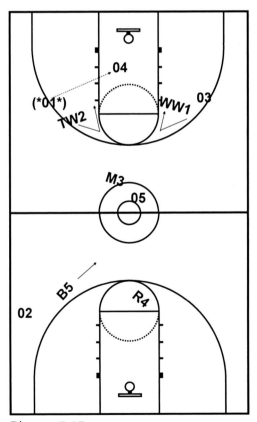

Diagram 5-15

the zone press, the out stunt, is back into play. The offense now has an even smaller window of time to cross the time line as more of their 10 seconds has been used in trying to read the defense's different and unexpected plan of attack.

Neither wing of the press (TW2 and WW1) should fully commit to the middle gap dribble for two basic reasons. The first reason is that you don't want two defenders to be guarding the ball at the same time in this area of the floor. The second reason is you do not want a defensive wing to get pulled into the middle of the gap and then be unable to control and contain the dribbler after a pass is made to the wing. The defense does not want that wing player to be able to dribble down his respective sideline. By not making that full commitment to the gap dribble, this gap dribbler (04) may be able to fully penetrate that gap between TW2 and WW1 (Diagram 5-16).

If there is a full penetrating dribble by 04, both TW2 and WW1 should be able to wolf the dribbler as M3 could become the new container and stalk the dribbler. M3 slows down and contains the dribbler as TW2 and/or WW1 attack the blind backside of the dribbler by sprinting down the middle of the floor to get to the new ball level and to protect their basket.

The defense has greatly influenced the opposition's offense into using one of its poorer ball handlers into making point guard decisions and handling the basketball. If 04 is fortunate enough to advance the ball up the middle of the court and survive wolf attempts by TW2 and WW1, R4 and B5 may have to tandem up to protect the basket as M3 stalks the dribbler and brings him under control. Regardless of how the offense attempts to survive the 2 press, the 3 press, or the 1 press, the defense has answers and countermeasures with their four defensive stunts.

The opposition's offense could possibly impel the 2 press to change the frequency of how often the out stunt is utilized if their sideline dribbler is outstanding and if they place an offensive receiver very deep and wide along the baseline. The designated defender (M3) that is to shoot the gap to intercept that sideline pass from the dribbler first has the primary responsibility of denying a penetrating pass to the middle of the zone press. Depending upon the distance between the offensive player located in the middle of the press and how far and wide the deep receiver in the ballside corner is, it might be asking too much for M3 to be able to consistently defend the middle and intercept or deflect that long sideline pass (Diagram 5-17).

In those instances when the opponent's ballside pass receiver locates in the very deep corner while an offensive teammate posts up in the middle, the out stunt may not be as effective as usual. Because of the distance M3 must travel when he first protects the middle and then shoots the gap toward the ballside corner pass receiver, an adjustment must be made defensively. The in or the stay stunts might be more effective and productive. Coaches must also keep in mind that just because an out stunt is called doesn't mean that either B5 or R4 must rotate up to trap the ball. B5 and R4 must feel the trap will be productive or they bluff and retreat. It must be remembered also that the continuity of the zone press also does not have to be the out stunt.

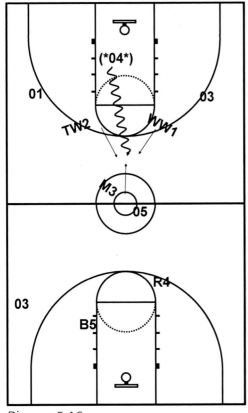

Diagram 5-16

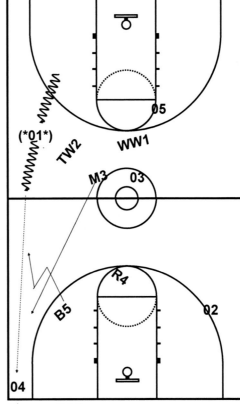

Diagram 5-17

It might be prudent for the coaching staff to evaluate its strategy of using the out stunt by keeping stats on the frequency and success rates of each press's various stunts, as well as the overall effectiveness of each zone press's package. Maybe the in stunt has not been executed enough to cause doubt and confusion in the ball handler's mind. Maybe the out stunt has been utilized too often and has become too predictable. The lack of success might be due to improper techniques such as whether the ball defender (TW2, in this scenario) or if the ballside defender rotating up (B5, in this instance) are executing their respective and necessary techniques properly. Possibly, M3 does not have the proper stance and positioning/location to be able to be consistently successful and is delayed in getting freed up from the middle of the press offense. Quite possibly, TW2 (or WW1 on the opposite side) are not putting enough ball pressure on the dribbler, allowing the ball handler to pick apart the defense as a good quarterback in football can do when he has all the time in the world to read the defense and make the proper decisions.

The ball defender (TW2 or WW1) must make the dribbler/passer more of a scrambling quarterback versus a quarterback that has plenty of time to make the proper decisions. The ball defender possibly must take more of the ball handler's attention and concentration. Perhaps the ballside sideline defender, B5, (in this case, or R4 on the opposite side) is not as deceptive as he should be when executing his bluff and retreat approach. Perhaps B5 and R4 are too predictable to the opposition's dribbler/passer. Maybe the designated sideline surprise trapper (B5 or R4) or the designated gap shooter (M3) are not aggressive-minded enough and afraid to make a mistake, causing them to be too cautious and therefore too slow. B5 (or R4) must change up their decision of when, if, and where to execute the jump trap on the ball. Perhaps M3 is not closely monitoring the rotation of either B5 or R4 and being equally aggressive with his own defensive rotation.

For whatever reason that M3 cannot consistently be successful in his shooting the gap rotation toward the sideline pass, the in stunt could possibly be used more often to supplement the out stunt. The other possibility would be to stress to the designated surprise trapper (B5 or R4 in each press's out stunt) to be more selective in his attempts to trap the basketball and thereby just have the ball defender fan the ball across the line and immediately initiate the half-court defense. Therefore there could be fewer traps, but fewer points scored by the opposition as a result of a gamble and missed interception (by M3). It also must be remembered that just because M3 misses the interception or because of other defensive breakdowns, good reactions and recoveries by all defenders to always hustle to get to the new ball level the opposition still has much work to do to score. The defense can afford to continue pressing if no easy scores are made on the unsuccessful stunts that have been executed. Or just apply the stay stunt a few times, and the offense might forget to attack the middle and the wide baseline corner. Diagram 5-18 shows the stay stunt being applied.

When Should a Team Full-Court Zone Press?

An obvious time to set up any of the possible three full-court presses would be to quickly do so after your team has just scored a field goal basket. Coaches can and should expect that all five defenders are able to quickly get into their original 1, 2, or 3 press locations/positions after a made basket. Remember, four defenders always go to the same spots regardless of the press; only M3's spot changes. This should be drilled and drilled and drilled until it is instinctive. Diagram 5-19 displays each defender hustling to get to their positions of the 2 press after the team has scored a basket.

Another opportunity to press takes a great deal of time and effort on both players and coaches to perfect, but the efforts could pay huge dividends. This scenario is on situations after missed field goals that are rebounded by the opposition. This situation is somewhat unique, and many opposing teams cannot or are not fully prepared to execute a full-court press offense after securing a defensive rebound. It is not a common practice and the opposition's personnel cannot be pre-set after they have played defense and then secured a defensive rebound. Diagram 5-20 shows the defenders hustling to their 2 press positions after a missed basket.

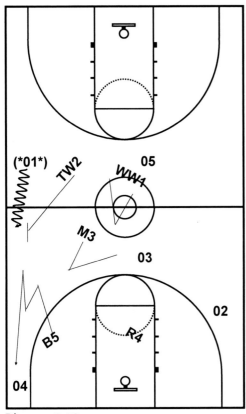

Diagram 5-18

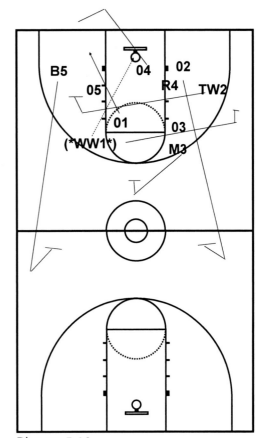

Diagram 5-19

A third opportunity that is much easier for the defense to execute is after the offense makes the last free throw that they shoot. Executing the press in this situation can be even more effective if the coaching staff and team can execute a substitution from the sideline after the last free throw shot is made. This substitution gives the pressing defensive team enough time to completely set up their personnel in the appropriate locations and organize their 1, 2, or 3 press defense as the sub(s) enter the game. This technique of subbing must be clearly understood and practiced by the defensive players to be completely utilized in the most effective manner.

The 3 press (with one of the particular four stunts) being called can be an additional devastating defensive weapon. In this hypothetical situation, the offense just made the last free throw, and X6 just substituted for the shooting guard (X2). Therefore, this player substitutes for X2, and X6 becomes the new tight wing on the defense's left side of the court (Diagrams 5-21 and 5-22).

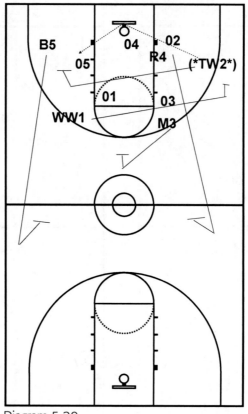

Diagram 5-20

A team that is committed to full-court zone pressing could utilize all three instances or situations just described, or only the two instances after their offensive team scores (field goals or free throws), or possibly just after free throw situations in which their team has just made the last free throw attempted.

It must be remembered that the more opportunities a defensive team presses, the more opportunities it gives itself to produce points off its full-court pressure defense. The more times that an opponent survives the press and the stunts but does not actually score gives the pressing defensive team more reason and more opportunities to actually press. The more opportunities a team presses, the more opportunities the defense has to cash in on turnovers and the opponents' poor decisions and overall offensive play.

A team that utilizes two or all three situations could also utilize various different original defensive alignments or at least different stunts that follow each of the three offensive scenarios. The specific offensive situations could be the signal and determine the specific stunt or defensive press desired by the coaching staff. This situation makes the pressure defensive system even more difficult to prepare against because of the opposition's uncertainty of when and if the defense will press, and what type of press

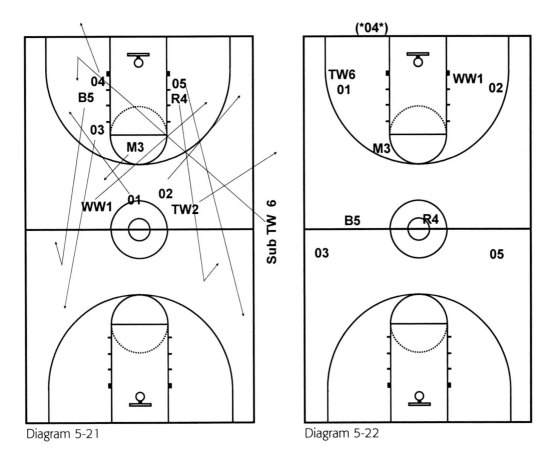

Diagram 5-21   Diagram 5-22

they will face. This situation also gives the defensive team another advantage of being the actors and forcing the opposition's offense to again become the reactors.

The aggressiveness and the attitude that the full-court press system gives to the defensive team a strong sense of confidence and a feeling of control. The uncertainty of the opposition as to not knowing when, where, and how the defense is going to attack them gives still another advantage to the defensive team. The defensive team can feed off of their confidence and aggressiveness to the point that it can carry over and allow them to have the same confidence and aggressiveness when executing its offenses.

Because of its four different stunts, the 2 press can be used the entire game. The 2 press can be a method of controlling the game's tempo. You can speed the game up with the in or out stunt, slow it down with the stay or match stunt, or confuse the opposition by mixing it up.

With the utilization of the four simple stunts, the 3 press can also be a multiple form of attack. This approach controls the tempo of the game as well as keeps the offensive opponent on its heels wondering when, if, where, and how their offense will be attacked.

If and when the 3 press is also integrated with one or both of the other zone presses, the defense becomes even more of a multiple force of attack. The full defensive press package is a great way to quickly overcome an inferior opponent. Your team must be up for the inferior opponent because the press compels aggressive movement that carries over to offense. A defensive team that uses this defensive scheme must mentally be prepared and never flat and not fully committed to playing any opponent.

When Should a Team Use or Not Use the Various Stunts?

The coaching staff must use the element of surprise to accomplish the goal of helping make his defensive team the actors and therefore force the opposition's offense to become the reactors. The element of surprise is a valuable commodity for that aggressive, defensive-minded coach. But, like anything else, too much of something is not always good. With experience, evaluation, and analysis (through having assistant coaches keep detailed stats during the game), a good coaching staff will learn when to use the press and when not to use the press. That coaching staff will know how often to use specific stunts and when not to use those same stunts. Following could be some examples of the various factors that could go into making the right strategy decisions.

Obviously, if the opposition is shredding the press and scoring off of the press and not just surviving the press, that coach must call the press or specific stunts off for the time being. That doesn't mean that he can't go back to it later. Most likely, a closer study and analysis can determine whether it is poor techniques and performances or a lack of hustle and intensity by defensive players or if the problem can be fixed with personnel moves, or a slight tweaking of the overall defense. Once the problems are identified and defined, they can most likely be rectified. From there, the (once unsuccessful) press (or stunts) can be reimplemented and oftentimes be met with surprising success. It remains a mystery why a defense or an offense can start out so poorly (or so well) in a game and later on in the same game can achieve an about-face in its overall performance and success. Coaches should remember in the same game to later on put on the press just for an occasional defensive possession to see if the press (or stunt) has regained its success. Specific instances of wise decision-making by a coaching staff could be any of the following, with experience showing a coach countless others:

- If the opposition has one of their bigger players inbound (trigger) the ball in an attempt to defeat the full-court press, the defensive team must be very aware of quick (and possibly long) throw-ins and must have a quick conversion from their offense to their (full-court press) defense. Once that possible problem is solved, sometimes executing the 3 press allows the defense to attack the probable poor passing skills and experience of their offensive Trigger. Utilizing the 3 press defense or not, if the opposition's offense does succeed, the defense should let the Trigger step inbounds and allow him to receive the return pass. Because the stunting defensive team has influenced the offense to take the ball out of their best ball handler's hands and into probably one of their weaker ball handler's hands, that very probable weakness must be identified and attacked. From there, the match stunt can be very successful with the defensive pressing team creating and maintaining a defensive mismatch with possibly several advantages going toward the defense.

- If the opposition has one of their better passers and decision-makers as their inbounder (Trigger), the 3 press defense could be used for two possible reasons. Quite possibly, the poorer ball handlers who have become the primary pass receivers may not have the experience or the skills to properly get open to receive the initial inbounds pass. Those potentially poorer pass receivers have only five seconds to get open and receive the inbounds pass before then facing other forms of defensive on-the-ball pressure. In addition, even if the opposition is fortunate enough to get the ball inbounds; the defense could then work hard on denying the return pass to their (possible best ballhandling) Trigger and thereby forcing the opposition to have a more inferior ball handler handle the ball.

- For basically the same reasons, if the opposition Triggers the ball with 01 or 02, it would be prudent to first execute the 1 press. This approach is to capitalize on double-team trapping an inferior ball handler (such as 03, 04, or 05) that is also close to the pressing team's offensive basket, making it highly possible for not only a turnover, but a quick score by the defensive team after creating the opposition's turnover.

- As previously mentioned, if the opposition uses the ballside deep corner (potential) pass receiver, this makes it difficult for M3 to be able to successfully shoot the gap for an interception during the execution of the out stunt. Instead, the stay stunt or the in stunt could be applied off and on with no sense of predictability to help confuse the offensive opponents and counter their revised measures.

- Defensive-minded coaches should use the stunts in a strategic and analytical way, while always keeping the opposition off-guard of when and how and which one is on the way.

Using any or all of the various four stunts with the three different presses can lead to a great deal of confusion on the opposition's offense and their plan of execution. With all of the stunts basically being the same with the same personnel in basically the same positions/locations, and with the same concepts, the same terminology, the same objectives and goals, the same required techniques, the defensive full-court press package can be as diverse, as complicated to the opposition, yet very simple to teach to your players.

If your defensive team can first learn how to always successfully get back to defend the basket and prevent easy scores if and when the opposition first survives the defensive attack, the defensive team can possibly have its most effective offensive attack in the form of its full-court zone press defensive package—and you can run it all night without fear of being beaten by a full-court press offense.

6

Press Defensive Breakdown Drills

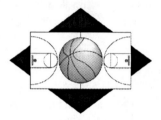

Presses and stunts can be taught and their execution perfected using breakdown drills. The drills that follow will give defensive players not only a working understanding and knowledge of the ins and outs of the presses, but a means for all players to hone in on the individual defensive techniques, methods, and skills that are vital for these presses to be successful.

Not only should the full-court press system be sold to the players, but the value of using drills to improve the full-court press system must also be sold to each and every player. All full-court defensive drills may be modified to fit a team's individual needs. The defensive drills presented in this chapter are the elementary breakdown drills that can be very beneficial to any pressing defensive team. These drills can fit whatever type of pressing defense a coaching staff would want his teams to run. A coaching staff can modify and adapt these basic drills to their own needs while creative defensive coaches can add on other drills to develop their own pressing system. Each coaching staff should remember the "A-B-C-D-E-F" points:

- *A*ssume those players know nothing.
- *B*e detailed in the teaching of the fine points and all of the techniques.

- *Criticize* in a positive manner and overlook nothing.
- *Demand* nothing but the greatest efforts and attention from all players.
- *Enthusiasm, Energy,* and *Example.* Coaches should always lead and show by example the high levels of enthusiasm and energy that are requisites for any press defenses to be successful.
- *Fundamentals, Fundamentals, Fundamentals.* Constantly work on the fundamentals of defense to form a foundation for the defense.

While many other drills can be created to fit the specific needs of a particular team, the following are full-court press breakdown drills:

- Push-push
- Pride
- Bluff and retreat breakdown
- Out trap stunt breakdown
- In trap stunt breakdown
- Match stunt breakdown
- 3-on-2 to 2-on-1 breakdown
- 2-on-1 breakdown
- 3-on-2 to 2-on-1 transition
- Gap dribble breakdown
- Gap dribble to out trap
- Shoot the gap interception breakdown
- Sprint and wolf breakdown
- Full-court zone press shell breakdown
- Defensive pride breakdown
  ✓ Starting with gap dribble
  ✓ Ending with take the charge
  ✓ Ending with loose ball
- Quick transition breakdown
- FT subbing and press breakdown
- Transition
  ✓ From half-court offense to full-court zone press defense
  ✓ From full-court zone press defense to instant offense
  ✓ From full-court zone press defense to instant offense back into zone press defense

Push-Push Breakdown Drill (Diagram 6-1)

This drill has traditionally been a group drill for man-to-man defensive teams. Because the full-court zone press defensive package incorporates many of the same concepts, theories, and techniques, this basic fundamental should be a staple in any zone press defensive scheme. Maximum pressure on the basketball and defensive overplays to control and contain the dribbler are key ingredients to success for all three of the zone presses. Coaches should emphasize that all players push off of their lead foot and leg when they must change directions. When there is a change in direction by the ball handler, the players must drop-step and then start pushing off of their new lead foot and leg. Coaches can point or actually dribble a ball to indicate what direction they want their defenders to push toward during the drill. After a designated number of pushes and changes of directions, the defenders can perform other defensive techniques. The defenders can be asked to perform certain skills at the conclusion of the killed dribble, such as cross-facing and tracing the (imaginary) ball, or boxing out an imaginary shooter.

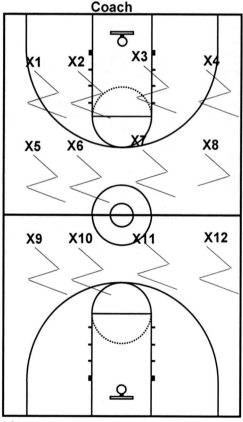

Diagram 6-1

Pride Breakdown Drill (Diagram 6-2)

This drill also has traditionally been a drill for man-to-man defensive teams, but full-court pressing teams should also use this vitally important defensive fundamental drill. As defenders become more efficient, the actual area that each individual defender is to defend should become more of a challenge and more realistic by getting wider as well as longer. At first, the dribbling area should end at the timeline, then later at the far free throw line, and, ultimately, at the far baseline. The width of the offensive dribbler's area should first begin with just the free throw lane area extended downcourt. After success by the defensive players, the next area should be widened so that the full court area is divided somewhat equally into two parts: the sideline to the nearest edge of the free throw lane (on both sides of the court.) The area could then be extended from the sideline to the far line of the free throw lane. The final defensive breakdown practice area is the entire width of the court (from sideline to sideline.) At any time in any of the designated dribbling lengths and widths of the practice, the dribblers can be held to less restrictions to make it more of a defensive challenge and more game-realistic.

The drill should begin with the defensive player in each line controlling and turning the dribbler. To add variety and to emphasize different aspects of the full-court pressing defenses, different defensive mechanics can be added to the drill, such as versus gap dribbles or out of a beaten/defeated situation. The ending points of the pride drill could include take the charge and loose ball. As previously discussed, one, two or three dribbling alleys (to save practice time) can be used for a maximum of three pairs of players to drill at the same approximate time. In Diagram 6-2, three lines are used to execute the fundamentals of this drill.

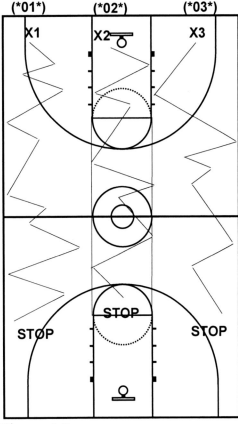

Diagram 6-2

Bluff and Retreat Breakdown Drill (Diagram 6-3)

This breakdown drill has two major objectives. First, the ball defender (TW2 or WW1) fans the dribbler to the outside. Second, the ball defender controls the dribbler down the sideline until the ballside second-line defender (B5 or R4) fakes coming up to trap before actually rotating up to double-team trap with the ball defender (either WW1 or TW2). This concept is called bluff (feigning the coming up to trap) and retreat (dropping back away from the fake trap). The actual trap should also be practiced being set on either side of the 10-second timeline. Diagram 6-3 shows the drill being executed on both sides of the floor. The use of both sides of the floor allows for more repetitions in the same amount of practice time, thus being time-efficient as well as space-efficient.

The trap should be set as close to the sideline as possible. TW2 or WW1, whichever is the defender on the dribbler, should narrow the dribbling alleys as the dribbler approaches the timeline. Both sides of the court could be used simultaneously for time and court space efficiency.

The drill can be organized in a controlled setting by limiting the actions of the offensive player. These conditions should first be practiced to give the edge to the defensive team, which helps develop confidence and skill levels of the defenders. As the defenders become more and more efficient, the conditions should be modified to make it a greater and greater challenge for the defensive team. The ideal final setting should be set up so that it is more of a challenge for the defense than it is in actual game settings.

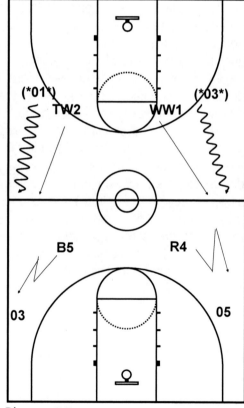

Diagram 6-3

Out Stunt Breakdown Drill (Diagram 6-4)

This specific drill also breaks down the techniques and methods needed for this out stunt to be effective. It really should have three objectives. First, the defender on the dribbler should control the dribbler and force the dribbler to the sideline. Second, the backline defender (B5 or R4) should bluff and retreat the dribbler (01 or 02) before then rotating up to trap the ball handler. Third, M3 should be watching the trappers, while working on shooting the gap techniques. M3 should make the interception or at least the deflection of the long sideline pass. Diagram 6-4 shows the drill being practiced on both sides of the court, which allows for more repetitions in the same amount of practice time.

Both sides of the court should be used in this drill for time and space efficiency. The drill can be organized in a controlled setting by limiting what the offensive players can do. After the defense feels comfortable, is more successful, and is ready for more of game-realistic challenge, then more offensive options can be drilled until all offensive options are available to the offense. This approach gives the defense more repetitions and eventually more confidence in their skill levels.

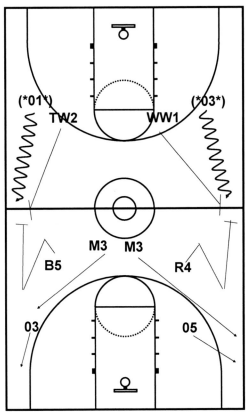

Diagram 6-4

In Stunt Breakdown Drill (Diagrams 6-5 and 6-6)

This particular drill breaks down and emphasizes the techniques and methods needed for the in stunt to be successful. Three areas need to be stressed. First, it focuses on the ball defender controlling the dribbler and forcing the ball down the sideline. Then, the defender on the dribbler must race ahead of the dribbler and force the dribbler to change directions, preferable with the spin dribble. Second, the backline defender on the ballside (B5 or R4) should bluff and retreat the dribbler before then staying back to deny the long sideline pass. In Diagram 6-5, both sides of the court are being used to execute the in stunt. Doing so allows for more repetitions in the same amount of practice time, so players can become more proficient in their execution of this valuable stunt.

When the ball defender gets ahead of the dribbler to turn him back into the middle, the middle defender (M3) surprise-jumps the dribbler to form a different type of double-team trap. The remainder of this breakdown drill specializes in the middle defender of the press (M3) reading his ball defender teammate turning the dribbler before then trapping the ball with the same proper trap techniques already taught and practiced in the other breakdown drills. Diagram 6-6 displays the drill being run to both sides of the court.

Two different middle defenders are used so that both sides of the full court can be used to save practice time. The drill can be organized in a controlled setting so that the offensive players are limited to just certain offensive options. After the defense has mastered those single options and gained greater confidence, the offense can be given more options to make the drill more challenging and more game-realistic to the defensive group.

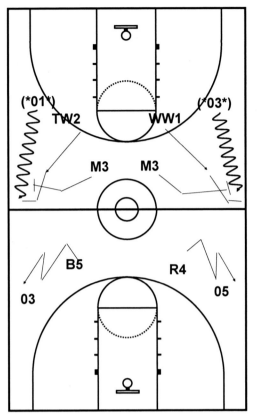

Diagram 6-5

Diagram 6-6

Match Trap Breakdown Drill (Diagram 6-7)

This breakdown drill teaches the defenders the tactics used in the match stunt. The drill begins with 01 with the basketball. 01 passes back to 05. The defense now has two types of coverage available. WW1 can rotate to cover the new receiver (05), or M3 can cover 05. Regardless, R4 would step up to cover whomever is posting up in the middle of the press, who in this case is 04. This variance in this part of the coverage must be decided before game time by the coaching staff and passed on to the players. Coaches should use scouting reports to determine the best match-up for individual defenders and for the overall success of the match stunt. Diagram 6-7 displays WW1 rotating to cover 05, but WW1 could easily stay in the middle as R4 steps up to take the offensive player in the middle, 05, while M3 slides over to cover 03.

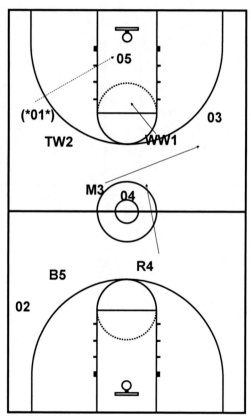

Diagram 6-7

3-on-2 to 2-on-1 Transition Breakdown Drill (Diagrams 6-8 through 6-11)

This full-court drill emphasizes offensive, defensive, and transition fundamentals both on the full- and the half-court phases of the game. OO1 passes the ball to OO2 and cuts behind the pass receiver, while OO3 angles toward the middle. OO2 passes the ball to OO3 and cuts behind him. It is a three-man weave until the ball approaches the offensive hash mark and then the three offensive players attack the two defenders (X4 and X5) in a 3-on-2 offensive/defensive situation. The two initial defenders (X4 and X5) both start in various locations in the backcourt as they would if they started as half-court offensive players. This positioning is to make their part of the drill as game-realistic as possible in that they must have to transition from the offensive half-court location before having to then sprint back to defend their own basket.

The defensive transition segment of the drill first emphasizes that the two new defenders in transition must sprint back to the top of the key and clearly communicate who becomes the top player and who is the bottom player in the vertical tandem that they must create to adequately protect their basket, while buying time for defensive reinforcements. It is important that the top defender (X4) is called the ball man, who

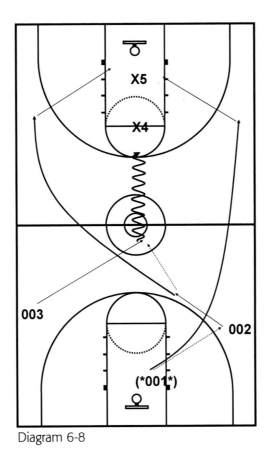

Diagram 6-8

stops the dribbler before then dropping quickly to the basket to become the new basket man once the first pass is made. The original basket man (X5) always takes the first pass (from 003 to 001 on the right side), regardless of where the pass is made. These two defenders have two goals: to prevent easy and quick scores and to buy their team some time for the remaining three defenders to get back on their transition defense (Diagram 6-9).

The original basket man (X5) actually always takes the first two passes, regardless of whether the initial wing pass is made to the left or the right side. If 001 receives the first wing pass (on the right side of the court) and has no open shot and reverses the ball back to 003, X5 must always take that second pass also. These two defenders have then done their job by preventing quick or uncontested shots and forcing two or more passes, which gives the remaining three defenders time to get back on their transition defense.

If the second wing pass is made to the left side (from 003 to 002), X4 (the new basket man) always takes that next wing pass and the following reversal pass, while the new ball man (X5) drops to become the next basket man (Diagram 6-10). This step

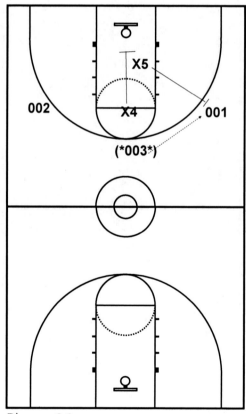

Diagram 6-9

concludes the 3-on-2 portion of this invaluable transition drill, which should be utilized regardless of whether the press package is decided upon or not.

Whichever offensive player (O01, O02, or O03) shoots the ball or commits the turnover offensively, that specific player is to be the new solo defender who must get back on defense at the opposite end and stop the 2-on-1 fast break. Both original defenders (X4 and X5) quickly start their conversion from defense to offense by staying wide and advancing the ball quickly (but under control) down the court in the opposite direction. Once in the "paint," the lone defender (O01, O02, or O03) must stay in the path between the original ball handler and the basket. That defender will align himself in a sideways stance with his outside foot up and his belly facing the potential pass receiver. Physically, he stops the ball, and mentally he is prepared to close out after the pass is forced to the other offensive player. (In Diagram 6-11, O02 is the defender because he took the shot in the 3-on-2 phase of the break.) This step concludes the 2-on-1 portion of the fast break.

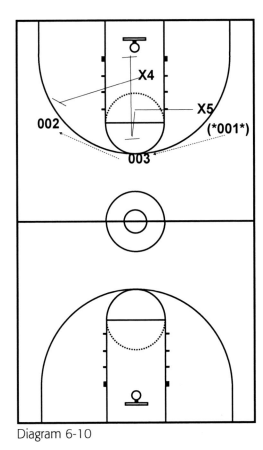

Diagram 6-10

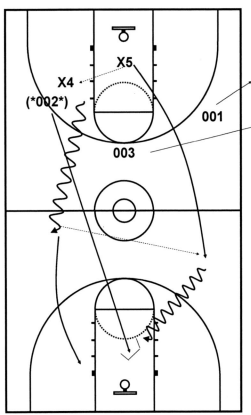

Diagram 6-11

Gap Dribble to Out Stunt Breakdown Drill (Diagrams 6-12 and 6-13)

This drill is used to teach the frontline defenders to stop the gap dribble yet recover on the pass back to the wing. This exercise is somewhat of an expanded version of the techniques used and the drill utilized to work on the half-court man-to-man defensive techniques traditionally called "help-and-recover" concept. The wing defender would want to stop the gap dribble, force the pass to the wing, and then control the new ball handler and force the dribble up the sideline. Then, the out stunt would commence. The two frontline defenders (TW2 and WW1) must stop the middle penetration. The gap dribbler, 04 in Diagram 6-12, would pass to either 01 or 03. If the pass goes to 01, TW2 must control 01 and force him to the outside (fan him). From there, the out stunt could be executed, particularly since the dribbler has the angle to drive down their particular sideline and is strongly influenced by the ball defender TW2 to continue in that direction. B5 will bluff and retreat until he eventually comes to set the trap with TW2.

The two frontline defenders (TW2 and WW1) can prevent the middle penetrating dribble. Once the dribble is stopped, both defenders must be ready to still contain and control the sideline dribble that is sure to come after the ball has been pitched out to either wing. From there, the two (new) ballside defenders on the defense's left side of the court (TW2 and B5) prepare to trap the ball down their sideline. This version is the out stunt except after the ball is reversed and re-reversed, B5 sets the trap with TW2 while M3 shoots the gap on the deep corner (Diagram 6-13).

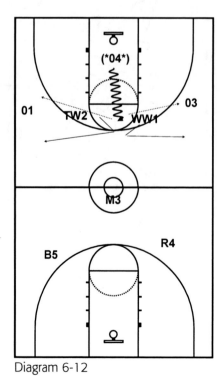

Diagram 6-12

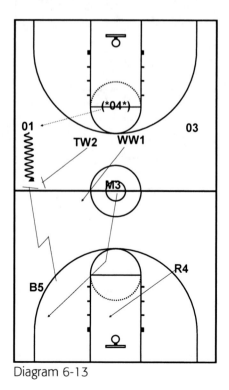

Diagram 6-13

Shoot the Gap Interception Drill (Diagram 6-14)

This drill also breaks down the techniques and methods needed particularly for the out stunt. This drill should be used and practiced probably more than the other breakdown drills, particularly if the out stunt is to become the defense's continuity attacking option. The ball defender (TW2 or WW1) controls and contains the dribbler by fanning the ball down their sideline. M3 denies the middle pass to a designated manager or an assistant coach. When the ballside backline defender (B5 or R4) stops his dancing in his bluff and retreat movements and finally rotates up to trap, M3 releases the middle and shoots the sideline gap, looking to intercept the long sideline vertical pass.

Both sides can again be utilized simultaneously for time and space efficiency. B5 and R4 both can work on their sideline trapping techniques with TW2 and WW1 respectively, with two different players refining their instincts, techniques, and skills by acting as the gap shooter (M3). Managers or assistant coaches could act as the press offense's two sideline pass receivers.

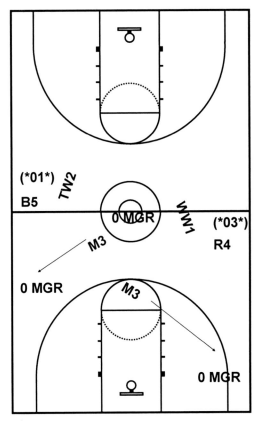

Diagram 6-14

Sprint and Wolf Drill (Diagram 6-15)

Sometimes, the dribbler escapes the lone ball defender or the double-team trap. Ideally, that should not happen often; but when it does, all defenders must sprint to get to the new ball level and stop the ball. The defenders closest to the dribbler should follow the dribbler from behind, hoping to wolf the ball (back-tip from behind). If the ball is not wolfed, the hustling defenders should then at least get ahead of the basketball to stop the advancement of the ball. In Diagram 6-15, TW2 and B5 have trapped 01 in presumably an out stunt that went bad. 01 splits the trap with a dribble. TW2 trails the dribbler on one side, and B5 trails the dribbler on the other side. Both try to steal (wolf) the ball from behind, forcing 01 to pick up his dribble. WW1 races back to get ahead of the ball to stalk and contain the dribbler. M3 and R4 get in a vertical tandem defense to protect the basket.

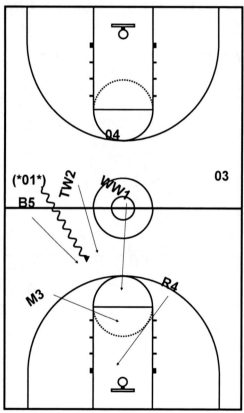

Diagram 6-15

Full-Court Shell Breakdown Drill (Diagram 6-16)

The traditional half-court shell drill is the most valuable defensive drill to teach man-to-man concepts and work on individual and overall team techniques. The same breakdown drill can be used to teach individual and team concepts of the zone press.

First, the full-court shell breakdown drill emphasizes both the proper location/position of each of the five defenders in relation to each individual's ball-you-man-in-your-zone-area flat triangle. After being comfortable with the positioning of each defender, the coach checks each of the five defender's stances. Stances are different for each defender. The defender on the ball has an overplay stance, designed to force the ball handler in the direction that he wants him to go. The off-the-ball defenders have more of denial or opened up to the ball stances. The farther each defender's man is from the ball, the farther that defender is from the man in his specific area. Each defender should point to the ball and point to the man in his area in a pistols stance with his head on a swivel. Every time the ball moves via a pass or dribble, each defender must adjust his flat triangle by jumping to the ball. The coaching staff should have the dummy offense pass the ball around and check the defensive stances and the defensive flat triangles of each defender before moving on to the next segment of the drill.

The next segment of the drill deals with the movement of the ball by dribble. The defender on the ball must keep the dribbler under control. The off-the-ball defenders anticipate a trap. The defender helping to set the trap with the ball defender must continually use the bluff and retreat techniques to prevent the opposition's dribblers from knowing when and if there is ever going to be a double-team trap on the dribbler.

The trap and the shooting-the-gap techniques practice and breakdown work should then follow. Coaches should observe, configure, and correct the stances and techniques of the trappers. They should make sure that the trappers form an L with their feet, that they cross-face and trace or mirror the ball, and that they correctly perform the other fine points and techniques. Coaches should make sure the gap shooter covers his assignment physically but is prepared mentally to shoot the gap. Coaching staffs should drill all players in this portion of the shell drill.

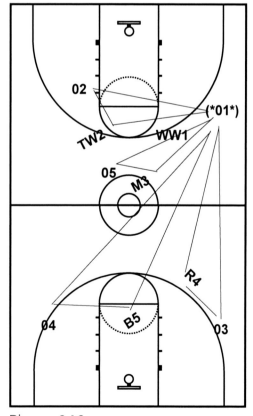

Diagram 6-16

Turnover Conversion Drills (Diagram 6-17)

The first of three types of transition drills should be game-realistic. The first type is the transition from half-court offense into one of the press defenses. The designated team could run a dummy offense versus a dummy defense. The dummy defense allows an uncontested score. Both teams then go live with the designated team immediately converting from offense to the designated full-court zone press defense. Once the ball is inbounded by the dummy team that is now on offense and the primary team is in a designated full-court zone press defense, coaches could stop the drill immediately, or they could continue to a designated point within the zone press defense (such as you have an out stunt called and you stop the drill on the ball reversal).

The second type of transition is for the defensive team to start in a specified zone press defense. The offensive team could intentionally surrender the ball in various forms of turnovers (such as fumbles or interceptions). When the defense obtains the ball from this turnover, they convert to instant offense. Diagram 6-17 shows 02 passing out of a trap. M3 intercepts the pass. M3 dribbles toward the middle of the court while his teammates instantly convert to an offensive fast break. Coaches would want to walk through this drill first before making it a live drill.

The third type of drill is to combine the two drills into one (controlled) drill. The primary team starts in a half-court offensive setting before they score against a dummy defense. The primary team instantly sets up in a designated full-court zone defense. The primary team would then obtain the ball with intentional turnovers against the new dummy press offensive team and work on scoring in a very short period of time. This drill is actually more game-realistic.

Breakdown drills improve all defenders in their understanding of the individual defensive concepts as well as the necessary techniques, slides, and assignments for the overall defensive team to improve. These drills should be constantly utilized and modified (as to degrees of difficulty) as the season progresses. The defense should face more difficult situations than they will encounter during a game.

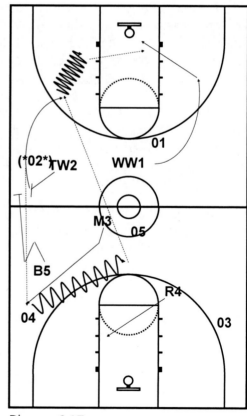

Diagram 6-17

Conclusion

The techniques, the slides, and the rotations of the zone press defenders, the fundamental language used in all three zone press defenses (the 3 press, the 1 press, and the 2 press) are all very comparable to each other. These three zone presses are three separate entities that could be used independently of each other, but the similar characteristics of the three zone presses makes teaching all of them simple, quick, and easy. Your players will spend less time and energy learning them, reviewing them, and practicing them than your opposition does on trying to prepare and solve them.

Confusion reigns in the opposition's offense and not your multiple defense. The opposition thinks they are facing a score of defenses and must prepare for each.

A defensive team can work on defensive skills needed for one specific zone press while working on a different zone press because all three zone presses have very similar attributes and characteristics. Very similar player techniques are used in each press and each stunt. The language and terminology are also identical. Defensive teams should utilize these advantages to the fullest degree, by using more than one press—if not all three—when possible.

Offensive-minded coaches usually attack this variety of full-court presses in different manners because of the major differences that each zone press possesses. The defense can use the same techniques to change the degrees of pressure, the types and locations of the traps, the pressure points, and the overall tempo and pace of the different presses. Incorporating various defensive stunts can confuse the opposition's offensive plan of attack even further. The various stunts can maximize defensive personnel's strengths and probably hide and/or minimize other particular defenders' weaknesses.

The 1-2-1-1 zone press (or the 1 press) is the most aggressive type of full-court zone press because of the immediately traps of the ball handler on the initial inbounded pass. Offensive opponents must counter this zone press in a different manner than the 2-1-2 (or the 2 press) because no immediate trap is set by the 2 press. In both cases, however, the offense will probably look to reverse the ball. When this happens, in both of these presses, the out stunt is immediately called (the continuity strategy).

The 1 press can be a forceful and aggressive defensive attacking plan, and the same stunts that work in the 2 press work in the 1 press.

The 2-1-2 press (or the 2 press) is more of a passive type of full-court zone press. It is generally a complementary press to the 1-2-1-1 full-court zone press, most likely the team's primary press. The 2-1-2 full-court zone press usually is more of a cautious and conservative press, attempting to lure the opposition's ball handler to dribble down the sideline before the trap is set. The setting of the trap can be on either side of the timeline with both locations having their own specific advantages and disadvantages.

The 2 press can be an effective way to create havoc on the opposition's offense as well as be a successful tool in controlling the overall tempo of the game. With the utilization of the stunts, the 2 press can remain a simple form of a defensive attack for the defense, while appearing to be very complicated and unpredictable to the opposition.

If the 2 press is utilized in conjunction with the 1 press, the defense becomes a multi-headed attack monster that can control the tempo of the game, create easy baskets for the pressing team, and prevent the opposition from flowing into its half-court offense.

The 3 press also is a zone press that has a distinct initial difference from the 1 or 2 press. The 3 press can fluctuate the degrees of pressure and the pressure points. The 3 press opens in face-guard pressure before the inbounds pass is even attempted. The 1 press's first pressure point is after the inbounds pass (the trap of the inbounds pass), and the 2 press's first pressure point is up near the midcourt line. The 3 press has as its first pressure point the trapping of the lob pass that the opposition's Trigger is forced to make because of the face-guarding denial pressure exerted by the front line. In all three zone presses, when the stay stunt is executed, none of the zone presses are really zone presses, but are actually man-to-man presses.

Defensive personnel are placed in locations where they can highlight their individual defensive skills. Quick guards play on-the-ball defense, while the best natural athlete plays as an interceptor. The biggest players are usually involved in setting traps, forcing the defense to throw lob passes over their (longer and) extended arms. Hiding possibly individual defender's weaknesses is manageable. For example, a coaching staff should place a slower player in the back line as B5 or R4.

Initial defensive alignments (of the 1 press or the 3 press) always evolve into the 2-1-2 zone press. If the press starts 1-2-1-1, it becomes a 2-1-2 press with the first reversal of the ball. The 2-1-2 zone press is the initial 2 press. The 3 press begins as a face-guard 2-1-2 aligned defense, but once the ball is entered into the backcourt; it also becomes the 2-1-2 zone press.

Now the stunts create even more confusion, yet they are very simple to learn. The reason is that all of the stunts are the same regardless of the initial press's alignment. The stunts offer various pressure points. In addition, one specific stunt (called the "match" stunt) even changes whatever zone press the defense is employing and morphs into a man-to-man full-court press.

The coaching staff can even change the strategy by changing the continuity stunt during the game. The continuity stunt is always the out stunt at the beginning. (Continuity stunts are always run after the first ball reversal.) By simply changing the continuity stunt from the out stunt to the stay stunt, you have completely changed the foundation of the press that is being executed.

Integrating the four stunts into all three zone presses gives the defensive team more of a multiple force of attack. It is most difficult for even the most sophisticated offenses to not be confused. This confusion often leads to instant offense by the pressing defense by forcing an opponent's turnover and a subsequent fast break.

About the Author

John Kimble began his basketball coaching career as an assistant basketball coach at Lexington (IL) High School. He was the head freshman coach, the head freshman-sophomore coach, and the assistant varsity basketball coach. During that season, each squad lost only two games and all three squads amassed an overall 61-6 record, with the varsity losing in overtime in the state tournament's Elite Eight round.

The following year, Kimble took the head basketball coaching position at Deland-Weldon (IL) High School, where the varsity accumulated a five-year record of 91-43 that included two regional championships, two regional runners-up, and one sectional tournament runner-up. From there, he moved to Dunlap (IL) High School. His five-year record at Dunlap amounted to an overall 90-45 record that included two regional runners-up, one regional championship, one sectional and one super-sectional championship, and a final 2nd place finish in the Illinois Class A State Tournament.

Kimble then moved to Florida, where he became an assistant basketball coach at Central Florida Community College in Ocala, Florida. The next year, he became the offensive coordinator in charge of the team's overall offense. For the next two years, he retained that offensive coordinator responsibility while also becoming the associate head basketball coach, with a two-year record of 44-22. The four-year overall record while at CFCC was 73-58.

Kimble then became the head basketball coach at Crestview (FL) High School for the following 10 years. Excluding the initial year, the overall record averaged almost 18 wins each year for the next nine years.

Kimble has worked close to 90 weeks of basketball camps and has spoken at several coaching clinics and camps. He also has had over 60 articles published in the following publications: *The Basketball Bulletin of the National Association of Basketball Coaches, The Scholastic Coach and Athletic Journal, Coach and AD, Winning Hoops,* and *Basketball Sense,* as well as contributing articles submitted and all diagrams drawn for the *The NABC's Coaching Basketball* in two separate editions.

Kimble has authored three other books published by Coaches Choice: *The Basketball Coaches' Complete Guide to Zone Offenses, The Basketball Coaches Complete Guide to the Multiple Match-Up Zone Defense,* and *Coaching Basketball's "Speed Game" With Primary and Secondary Fast Breaks.* He has also made four different series of DVDs on various topics of the game.

After 25 years of coaching basketball and several years of coaching baseball and football, Kimble is currently teaching business classes at Crestview (FL) High School, still studying the game, and still writing various basketball articles and books.